912

page 8

pages 10-11

pages 12-13

pages 14-15

pages 16-17

pages 42-43

A DORLING KINDERSLEY BOOK

Project Editor Donna Rispoli
Art Editor Lesley Betts

Managing Cartographer James Mills-Hicks

Cartography James Anderson, Caroline Bowie,
Tony Chambers, Yak EL-Droubie

Series Editors Sarah Miller, Sarah Phillips
Series Art Editor Eljay Crompton

Picture Researcher Becky Halls
Production Manager Ian Paton

Design Director Ed Day
Publisher Jonathan Reed

First published in Great Britain in 1994
by Dorling Kindersley Limited
9 Henrietta Street
London WC2E 8PS

Reprinted 1997

A CIP catalogue record for this
book is available from the British Library.

ISBN 0-7513-5117-2
Reproduced by Colourscan, Singapore
Printed and bound in Italy by Graphicom

Newton Primary School

ATLAS
OF THE
WORLD

DORLING KINDERSLEY
LONDON • NEW YORK
STUTTGART

CONTENTS

THE NATURAL WORLD 4

THE HUMAN WORLD 6

THE ARCTIC & ANTARCTICA 8

CANADA 10

THE UNITED STATES 12

CENTRAL AMERICA &
THE CARIBBEAN 14

SOUTH AMERICA 16

NORTHERN AFRICA 18

SOUTHERN AFRICA 20

NORTHERN EUROPE 22

WESTERN EUROPE 24

CENTRAL EUROPE 26

EASTERN EUROPE 28

THE MIDDLE EAST 30

NORTH & CENTRAL ASIA 32

THE INDIAN SUBCONTINENT 34

EAST ASIA 36

SOUTHEAST ASIA 38

AUSTRALIA 40

NEW ZEALAND &
THE PACIFIC ISLANDS 42

INDEX & GLOSSARY 44

HOW TO USE THIS ATLAS

Each map is coloured, full of place names and packed with different symbols, such as red dots and blue lines. The two keys on this page will help you work out what these colours and symbols mean. You can also learn how to use the index at the back of the book to find places on the maps.

Interesting natural regions, such as deserts and plateaus, are named on the map.

WHAT THE COLOURS MEAN

- Snow and ice
- Tundra
- Coniferous forest
- Temperate forest
- Temperate rainforest
- Mediterranean vegetation
- Temperate grassland
- Cold desert
- Hot desert
- Tropical forest
- Tropical rainforest
- Tropical grassland
- Mountains
- Wetland

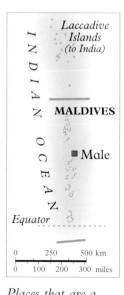

Places that are a long way from the mainland are put in a separate box.

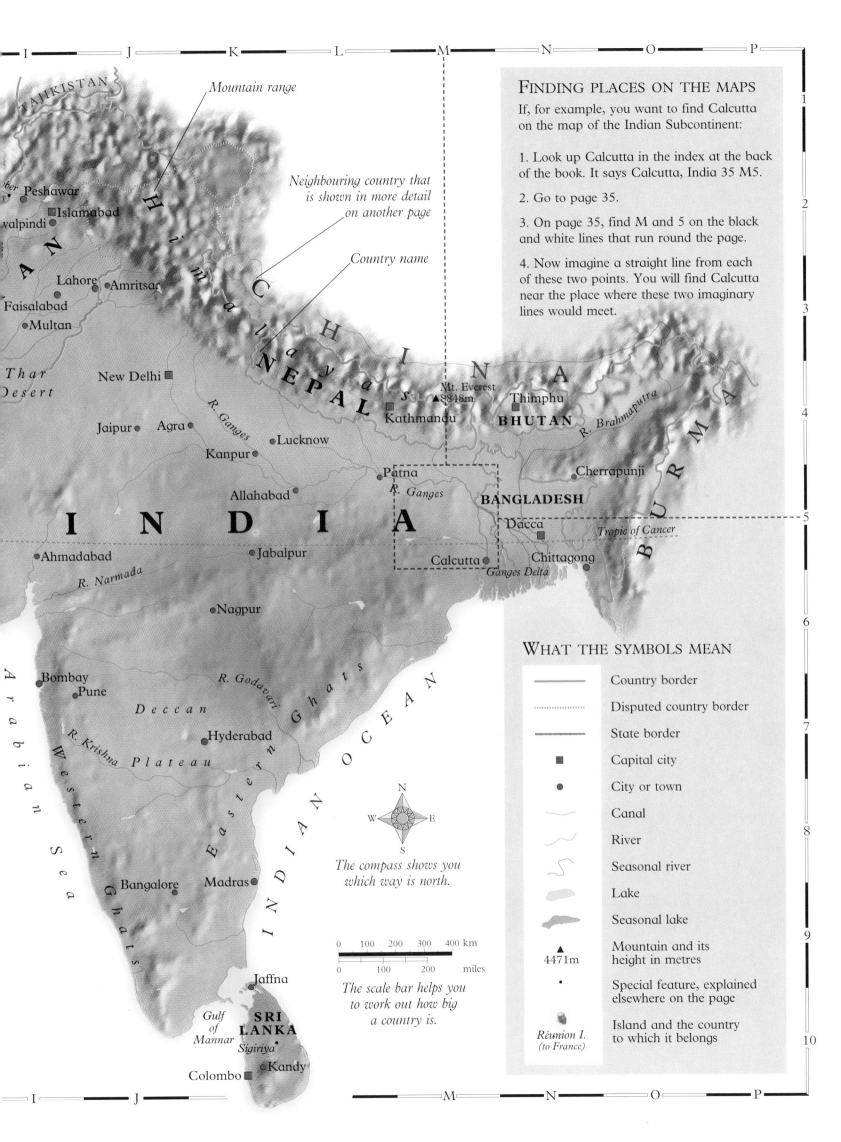

TAJIKISTAN

Mountain range

Peshawar

Islamabad

Rawalpindi

Neighbouring country that
is shown in more detail
on another page

Country name

Lahore   Amritsar

Faisalabad

Multan

*Thar
Desert*

New Delhi

C H I N A

NEPAL

Mt. Everest
▲8848m

Thimphu

Kathmandu

BHUTAN

R. Brahmaputra

B U R M A

Jaipur   Agra

Lucknow

Kanpur

R. Ganges

Patna

Cherrapunji

Allahabad

R. Ganges

BANGLADESH

I N D I A

Dacca

Tropic of Cancer

Ahmadabad

R. Narmada

Jabalpur

Calcutta

Chittagong

Ganges Delta

Nagpur

Bombay

Pune

R. Godavari

Eastern Ghats

Deccan

R. Krishna

Plateau

Hyderabad

*A
r
a
b
i
a
n

S
e
a*

*W
e
s
t
e
r
n

G
h
a
t
s*

I N D I A N   O C E A N

Bangalore   Madras

N
W   E
S

*The compass shows you
which way is north.*

Jaffna

*Gulf
of
Mannar*

**SRI
LANKA**

Sigiriya

Kandy

Colombo

				km
0	100	200	300	400 km
0	100	200		miles

*The scale bar helps you
to work out how big
a country is.*

FINDING PLACES ON THE MAPS

If, for example, you want to find Calcutta
on the map of the Indian Subcontinent:

1. Look up Calcutta in the index at the back
of the book. It says Calcutta, India 35 M5.

2. Go to page 35.

3. On page 35, find M and 5 on the black
and white lines that run round the page.

4. Now imagine a straight line from each
of these two points. You will find Calcutta
near the place where these two imaginary
lines would meet.

WHAT THE SYMBOLS MEAN

—————	Country border
·············	Disputed country border
—————	State border
■	Capital city
●	City or town
∿	Canal
∿	River
∿	Seasonal river
▬	Lake
▬	Seasonal lake
▲ 4471m	Mountain and its height in metres
·	Special feature, explained elsewhere on the page
*Réunion I.
(to France)*	Island and the country to which it belongs

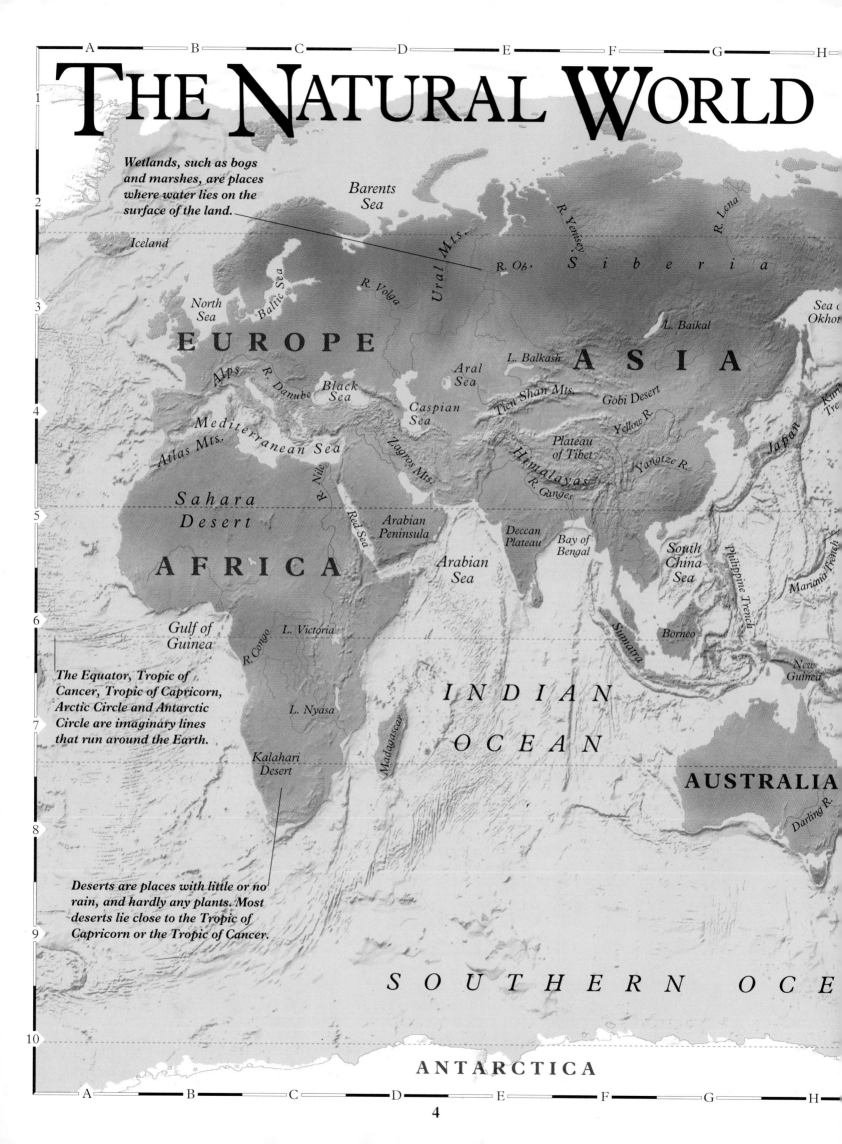

THE NATURAL WORLD

Wetlands, such as bogs and marshes, are places where water lies on the surface of the land.

Iceland

Barents Sea

North Sea

Baltic Sea

R. Volga

Ural Mts.

R. Ob

Siberia

R. Yenisey

R. Lena

Sea of Okhotsk

E U R O P E

Alps

R. Danube

Black Sea

Aral Sea

L. Balkash

L. Baikal

A S I A

Caspian Sea

Tien Shan Mts.

Gobi Desert

Mediterranean Sea

Atlas Mts.

R. Nile

Zagros Mts.

Yellow R.

Plateau of Tibet

Yangtze R.

Japan

Kuril Trench

Sahara Desert

Red Sea

Arabian Peninsula

Himalayas

R. Ganges

Deccan Plateau

Bay of Bengal

South China Sea

Philippine Trench

A F R I C A

Arabian Sea

Mariana Trench

Gulf of Guinea

R. Congo

L. Victoria

Sumatra

Borneo

New Guinea

The Equator, Tropic of Cancer, Tropic of Capricorn, Arctic Circle and Antarctic Circle are imaginary lines that run around the Earth.

L. Nyasa

Madagascar

I N D I A N

O C E A N

AUSTRALIA

Kalahari Desert

Darling R.

Deserts are places with little or no rain, and hardly any plants. Most deserts lie close to the Tropic of Capricorn or the Tropic of Cancer.

S O U T H E R N   O C E A

ANTARCTICA

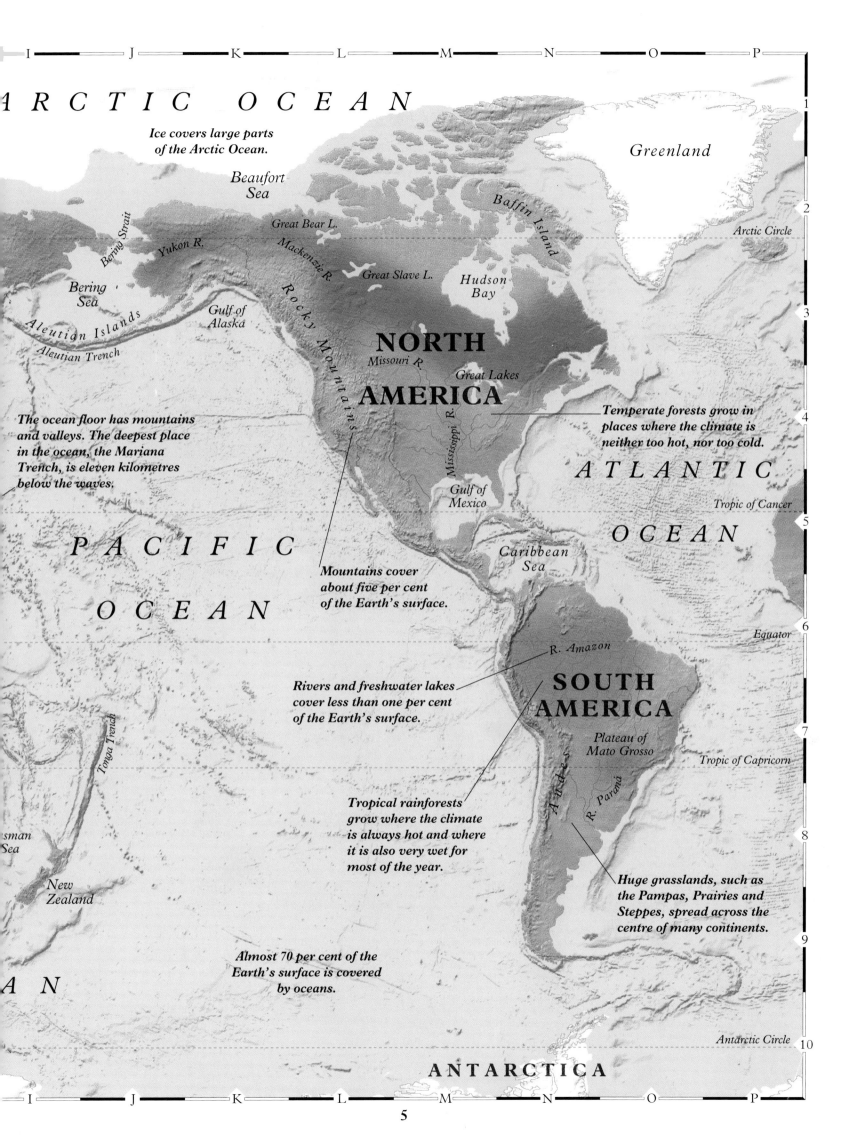

ARCTIC OCEAN

Ice covers large parts of the Arctic Ocean.

Greenland

Beaufort Sea

Baffin Island

Arctic Circle

Bering Strait

Great Bear L.

Yukon R.

Mackenzie R.

Bering Sea

Great Slave L.

Hudson Bay

Aleutian Islands

Gulf of Alaska

Rocky Mountains

NORTH AMERICA

Missouri R.

Great Lakes

Aleutian Trench

Temperate forests grow in places where the climate is neither too hot, nor too cold.

A T L A N T I C

The ocean floor has mountains and valleys. The deepest place in the ocean, the Mariana Trench, is eleven kilometres below the waves.

Mississippi R.

Gulf of Mexico

Tropic of Cancer

P A C I F I C

O C E A N

Mountains cover about five per cent of the Earth's surface.

Caribbean Sea

Equator

R. Amazon

Rivers and freshwater lakes cover less than one per cent of the Earth's surface.

SOUTH AMERICA

Plateau of Mato Grosso

Tropic of Capricorn

sman Sea

Tropical rainforests grow where the climate is always hot and where it is also very wet for most of the year.

Andes

R. Paraná

Tonga Trench

New Zealand

Huge grasslands, such as the Pampas, Prairies and Steppes, spread across the centre of many continents.

A N

Almost 70 per cent of the Earth's surface is covered by oceans.

Antarctic Circle

ANTARCTICA

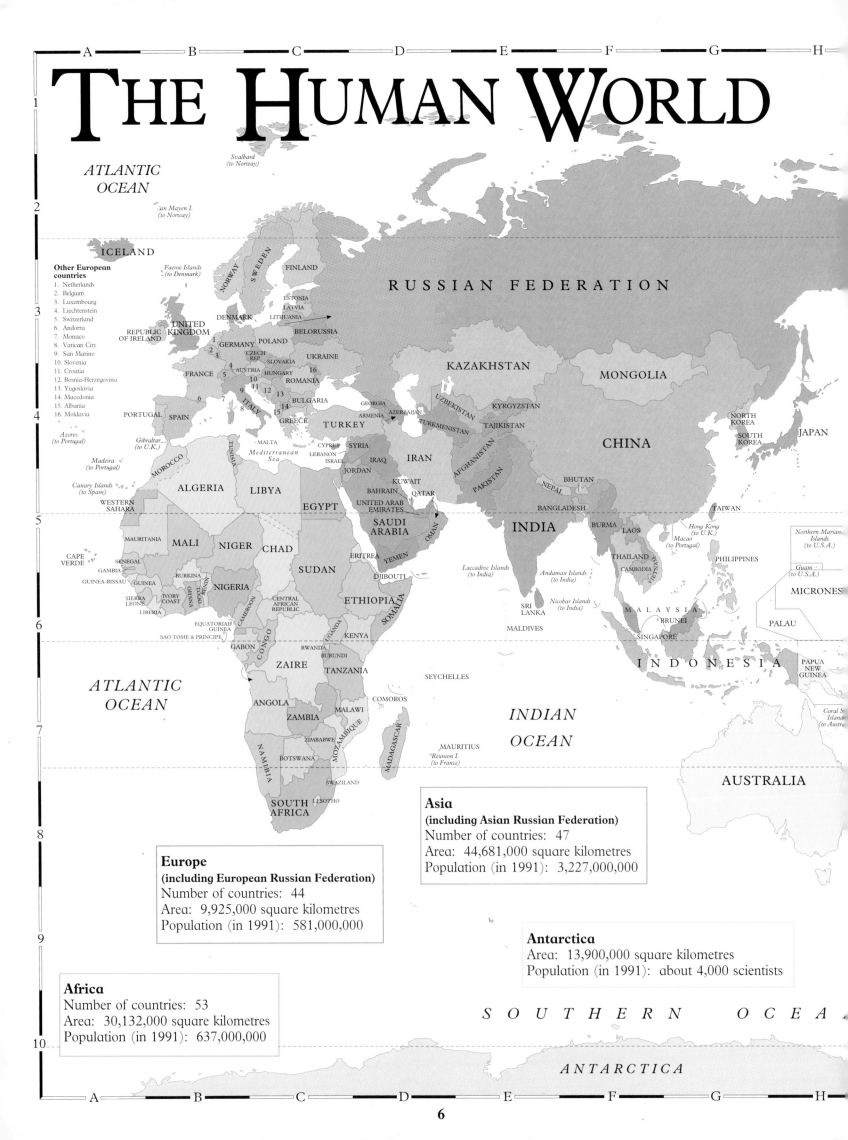

THE HUMAN WORLD

Europe
(including European Russian Federation)
Number of countries: 44
Area: 9,925,000 square kilometres
Population (in 1991): 581,000,000

Asia
(including Asian Russian Federation)
Number of countries: 47
Area: 44,681,000 square kilometres
Population (in 1991): 3,227,000,000

Antarctica
Area: 13,900,000 square kilometres
Population (in 1991): about 4,000 scientists

Africa
Number of countries: 53
Area: 30,132,000 square kilometres
Population (in 1991): 637,000,000

The Earth
Number of continents: 7
Area of land: 149,400,000 square kilometres
Area of ocean: 368,000,000 square kilometres
Population (in 1991): 5,184,000,000
Country with highest population
  (in 1991): China, 1,150,000,000

ARCTIC OCEAN

Greenland
(to Denmark)

1

2

Arctic Circle

Alaska
(to U.S.A.)

CANADA

3

*ATLANTIC
OCEAN*

**UNITED STATES
OF AMERICA**

4

*A continent is a large area
of land. North America, like
Antarctica and Africa, is
one of the seven continents.*

*Bermuda
(to U.K.)*

MEXICO

BAHAMAS

Tropic of Cancer

5

*Hawaii
(to U.S.A.)*

CUBA

*Puerto Rico
(to U.S.A.)*

DOMINICAN
REPUBLIC

HAITI

ANTIGUA & BARBUDA

DOMINICA

JAMAICA

ST. KITTS
& NEVIS

ST. LUCIA

**MARSHALL
ISLANDS**

BELIZE

*Caribbean
Sea*

BARBADOS

GUATEMALA HONDURAS

ST. VINCENT &
THE GRENADINES

EL SALVADOR

GRENADA

NICARAGUA

TRINIDAD & TOBAGO

COSTA RICA

SURINAM

NAURU

PANAMA

VENEZUELA

GUYANA

*French
Guiana
(to France)*

*Galapagos Islands
(to Ecuador)*

COLOMBIA

Equator

6

KIRIBATI

ECUADOR

*Tokelau
(to N.Z.)*

SOLOMON
ISLANDS

TUVALU

WESTERN
SAMOA

*American
Samoa
(to U.S.A.)*

PACIFIC OCEAN

BRAZIL

VANUATU

*Wallis & Futuna
(to France)*

*Cook Islands
(to N.Z.)*

PERU

7

*Niue
(to N.Z.)*

*New Caledonia
(to France)*

FIJI

TONGA

*French Polynesia
(to France)*

BOLIVIA

*Pitcairn
Islands
(to U.K.)*

PARAGUAY

Tropic of Capricorn

*Easter I.
(to Chile)*

**NEW
ZEALAND**

URUGUAY

*ATLANTIC
OCEAN*

8

North America
Number of countries: 23
Area: 24,134,000 square kilometres
Population (in 1991): 411,000,000

CHILE ARGENTINA

*Chatham Island
(to N.Z.)*

*Auckland Islands
(to N.Z.)*

*Falkland Islands
(to U.K.)*

9

South America
Number of countries: 12
Area: 17,820,000 square kilometres
Population (in 1991): 301,000,000

**Australia, New Zealand
and the Pacific Islands**
Number of countries: 14
Area: 8,808,000 square kilometres
Population (in 1991): 27,000,000

*South Orkney Islands
(to U.K.)*

Antarctic Circle

10

ANTARCTICA

THE ARCTIC & ANTARCTICA

The areas around the North and South Poles, which lie on opposite sides of the planet, are covered in ice. Although they look alike, these areas are very different. The Arctic, in the north, is a frozen ocean surrounded by land. Antarctica, however, is a vast area of land surrounded by an ocean. This southern icy region is almost twice the size of Australia. It is one of Earth's great landmasses, or continents.

The Arctic Ocean is the smallest of the Earth's oceans.

Arctic Circle

Bering Strait

RUSSIAN FEDERATION

ALASKA (to U.S.A.)

Wrangel I.

Beaufort Sea

Limit of Permanent Pack Ice

New Siberian Islands

Banks I.

Laptev Sea

ARCTIC OCEAN

Queen Elizabeth Islands

Limit of Permanent Pack Ice

Severnaya Zemlya

CANADA

North Pole

Kara Sea

Ellesmere I.

Franz Josef Land

Baffin I.

Thule

Barents Sea

Baffin Bay

Svalbard (to Norway)

Longyearbyen

Davis Strait

Greenland (to Denmark)

Greenland Sea

Godthâb

Arctic Circle

Denmark Strait

Cape Farvel

ATLANTIC OCEAN

Icy Marvel
Icebergs are pieces of floating ice. This iceberg is off Cape Farvel in Greenland. It looks big, but you can't see how huge it really is since 90 per cent of it is under the water.

Greenland is an enormous island. It is four times larger than France.

0   200   400   600   800   1000 km

0   200   400   600 miles

Green Summer
Low-growing tundra plants brighten up the coastal edges of icy Greenland. Grasses, mosses and lichen carpet these areas.

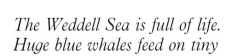

Pack of Ice
In July, during Antarctica's winter, the seas around the mountainous Antarctic Peninsula can freeze as far as 2,000 kilometres from the land. This frozen sea is called pack ice.

The Ice Life
Many of the animals that live in these freezing lands have a thick layer of fat under their skin to protect them from the bitter cold.

Arctic Animals

Polar bear

Walrus

0 200 400 600 800 1000 km

0   200   400   600   miles

The Weddell Sea is full of life. Huge blue whales feed on tiny creatures called krill.

SOUTHERN OCEAN

South Orkney Islands (to U.K.)

South Shetland Islands (to U.K.)

Anvers I.

Antarctic Circle

Antarctic Circle

Antarctic Peninsula

Weddell Sea

Bellingshausen Sea

Peter Ist I. (to Norway)

Ronne Ice Shelf

Ellsworth Mts.

Transantarctic Mountains

Queen Maud Land

Enderby Land

ANTARCTICA

SOUTH POLAR PLATEAU

Lambert Glacier

Davis Sea

South Pole
Amundsen-Scott (Research Station)

Amundsen Sea

Marie Byrd Land

Victoria Land

Ross Ice Shelf

Scott Base (Research Station)

Mt. Erebus 3794m

Ross Sea

Cape Adare

Wilkes Land

Vostok (Research Station)

The lowest temperature ever recorded on Earth was at Vostok. It fell to -89.2°C.

Antarctic Animals

Emperor penguin

Mount Erebus is a volcano. It sometimes throws out pieces of boiling lava onto the snow.

SOUTHERN OCEAN

An ice sheet is made of snow that fell millions of years ago.

Sea Shelf
In winter, the thick layer of ice that covers Antarctica spreads so much it spills onto the sea to form a shelf of floating ice. The Ross Ice Shelf is as high as the Eiffel Tower.

Blue whale

CANADA

The enormous country sandwiched between the United States and the Arctic is called Canada. Thousands of years ago much of this land was covered by ice, which carved out features such as the Great Lakes – the largest system of lakes on Earth. Today the climate is warmer and forests and grasslands spread over much of Canada. Ice still covers many of the islands in the far north.

Coast to Coast

The conifer trees growing by this lake in Alberta are part of an enormous forest that stretches across Canada. These tough trees can cope with a wide range of climates, from freezing cold winters to hot summers.

The Rocky Mountains form a long chain of peaks from Canada, through the United States, to Mexico.

Canadian Creatures

Moose

Grizzly bear

Timber wolf

North American porcupine

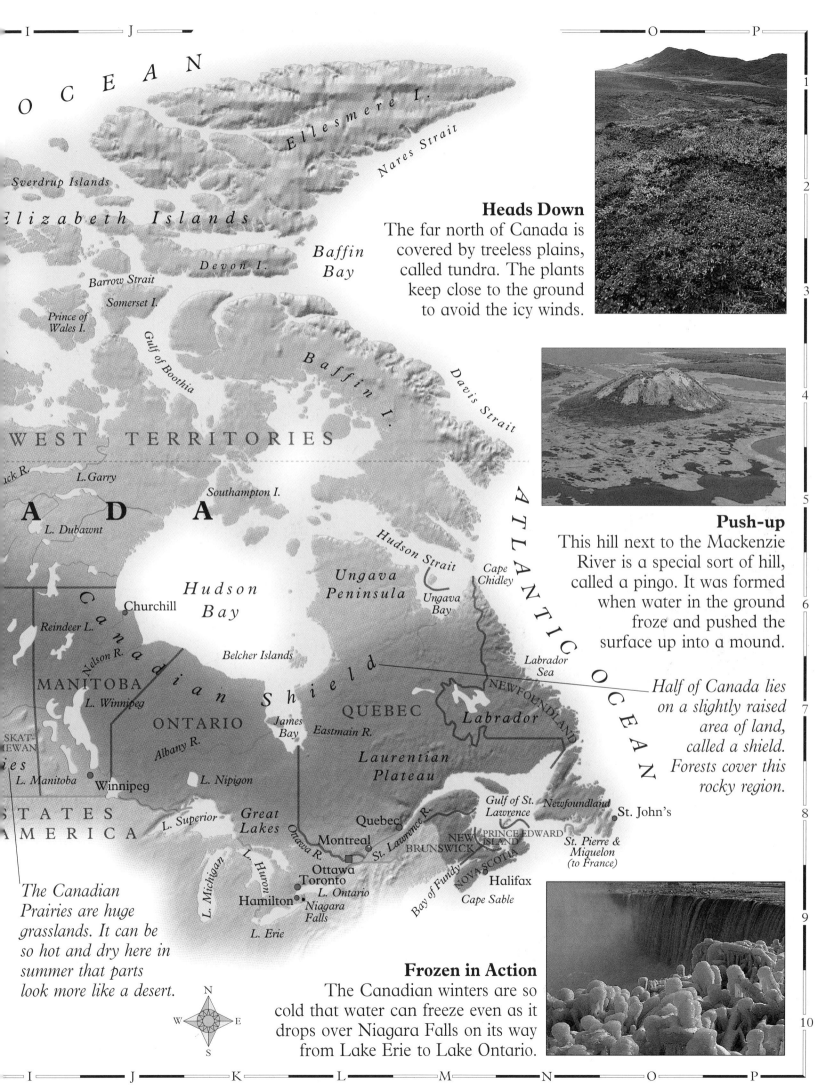

Heads Down
The far north of Canada is covered by treeless plains, called tundra. The plants keep close to the ground to avoid the icy winds.

Push-up
This hill next to the Mackenzie River is a special sort of hill, called a pingo. It was formed when water in the ground froze and pushed the surface up into a mound.

Half of Canada lies on a slightly raised area of land, called a shield. Forests cover this rocky region.

The Canadian Prairies are huge grasslands. It can be so hot and dry here in summer that parts look more like a desert.

Frozen in Action
The Canadian winters are so cold that water can freeze even as it drops over Niagara Falls on its way from Lake Erie to Lake Ontario.

THE UNITED STATES

The climate in the United States is very varied – Alaska in the far north is icy cold, yet Florida in the south is tropical. However, most of this region has a milder climate. The vast open spaces in the middle of this massive country are filled by grasslands, called the Prairies and Great Plains. In the west, the land rises up to form the mighty Rocky Mountains. The huge, hot deserts in the southwest of the country contrast with the cool, temperate forests along the east coast.

Beaver

The United States is made up of 50 states. Two of these, Alaska and Hawaii, are separated from the rest. Alaska lies next to northwest Canada. Hawaii lies 3,700 kilometres off the west coast of mainland United States.

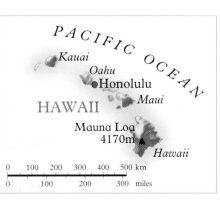

High and Dry

Flat-topped towers of rock, called buttes, stand on the hot desert floor of Monument Valley. They are the remains of a large plateau that has been worn away.

All American Mammals

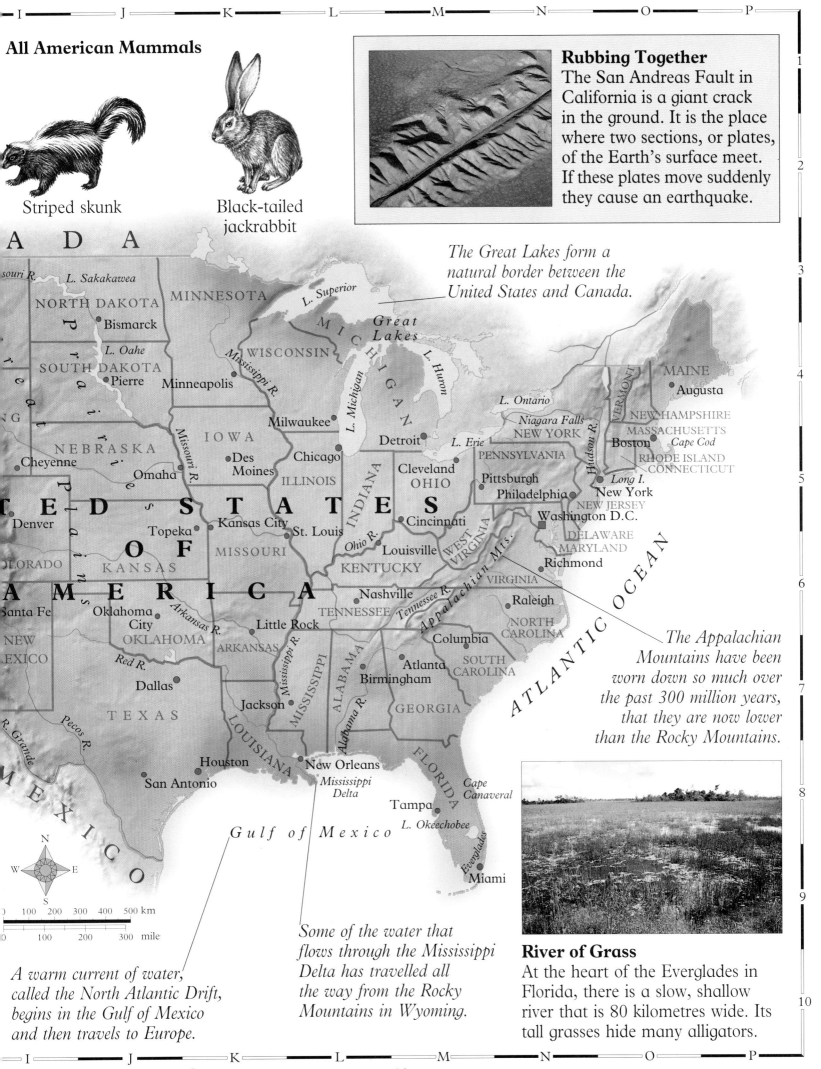

Striped skunk

Black-tailed jackrabbit

Rubbing Together
The San Andreas Fault in California is a giant crack in the ground. It is the place where two sections, or plates, of the Earth's surface meet. If these plates move suddenly they cause an earthquake.

The Great Lakes form a natural border between the United States and Canada.

The Appalachian Mountains have been worn down so much over the past 300 million years, that they are now lower than the Rocky Mountains.

A warm current of water, called the North Atlantic Drift, begins in the Gulf of Mexico and then travels to Europe.

Some of the water that flows through the Mississippi Delta has travelled all the way from the Rocky Mountains in Wyoming.

River of Grass
At the heart of the Everglades in Florida, there is a slow, shallow river that is 80 kilometres wide. Its tall grasses hide many alligators.

CANADA

Missouri R. · L. Sakakawea

NORTH DAKOTA · MINNESOTA · L. Superior

Bismarck

L. Oahe

SOUTH DAKOTA · Pierre · Minneapolis · Mississippi R. · WISCONSIN

Great Lakes

MICHIGAN · L. Huron

MAINE · Augusta

Milwaukee · L. Michigan · Detroit · L. Ontario · Niagara Falls · NEW HAMPSHIRE

NEBRASKA · IOWA · Chicago · L. Erie · NEW YORK · MASSACHUSETTS · Cape Cod

Cheyenne · Des Moines · ILLINOIS · INDIANA · Cleveland · OHIO · Pittsburgh · Boston · RHODE ISLAND · CONNECTICUT

Omaha · Hudson R. · Long I.

UNITED STATES · Denver · Kansas City · St. Louis · Cincinnati · Philadelphia · New York

Topeka · MISSOURI · Ohio R. · Louisville · WEST VIRGINIA · Washington D.C. · NEW JERSEY

OF · KANSAS · KENTUCKY · DELAWARE · MARYLAND

COLORADO

AMERICA · Nashville · Richmond

Santa Fe · Oklahoma City · Arkansas R. · Little Rock · TENNESSEE · Tennessee R. · Appalachian Mts. · VIRGINIA · Raleigh

NEW MEXICO · OKLAHOMA · ARKANSAS · Columbia · NORTH CAROLINA

Red R. · Mississippi R. · ALABAMA · Atlanta · SOUTH CAROLINA

Dallas · Jackson · Birmingham

Pecos R. · TEXAS · MISSISSIPPI · Alabama R. · GEORGIA

R. Grande · LOUISIANA · FLORIDA · Cape Canaveral

Houston · New Orleans · Mississippi Delta

San Antonio · Tampa · L. Okeechobee

MEXICO · Gulf of Mexico · Everglades · Miami

ATLANTIC OCEAN

N · W · E · S

100 200 300 400 500 km

100 200 300 mile

CENTRAL AMERICA & THE CARIBBEAN

The narrow strip of land connecting the United States to South America is known as Central America. All the way along this land bridge there are chains of mountains and active volcanoes. In the north there are cool, high plateaus and hot, dry deserts. It is wet enough farther south for tropical rainforests. The warm Caribbean waters that wash the southeast coast of this region contain two groups of tropical islands, the Greater and Lesser Antilles, often called the Caribbean islands.

UNITED STATES OF AMERICA

Tijuana

Ciudad Juárez

Sonoran Desert

Guadalupe I.

Cedros I.

Lower California

Gulf of California

Chihuahua

R. Conchos

R. Grande

Sierra Madre

Mexican Plateau

Falcon L.

Torreón

Monterrey

MEXICO

Marías Islands

R. Panuco

León

Guadalajara

L. Chapala

Mexico City

Puebla

Popocatépetl ▲ 5452m

Citlalté 5700r

R. Balsas

Acapulco

PACIFIC OCEA

Standing on Stilts
Mangrove trees grow along the hot, wet coasts of the Greater and Lesser Antilles. Their weird-looking roots trap mud and so help to stop the coast from being washed away by the sea.

Nearly every place along the west side of Central America has been affected by an earthquake or volcano at some time.

0 100 200 300 400 500 km

0 100 200 300 miles

N
W — E
S

Hot Spots
Hot deserts, such as the Sonoran, cover much of northern Mexico. These dry lands are dotted with cacti – prickly plants that survive by storing water in their swollen stems.

Valuable Discoveries

Many tasty foods were first grown in this region.

Red pepper (Capsicum)　Avocado　Red sweet potato　Maize

Blowing in the Wind

Beaches in the Dominican Republic, like most Caribbean coasts, are fringed with palms. These trees bend easily so they survive very strong winds, such as hurricanes, which blast over these islands.

The Great Bahama Bank is a huge sandy ridge under the sea.

Pitch In

Things that fall into this lake on the island of Trinidad meet a sticky end! Thick, black asphalt, the substance that is used to build roads, slowly flows into the lake from under the ground.

Thick tropical rainforests stretch from the Yucatán Peninsula, through the southern half of Central America and into South America.

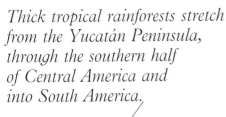

The Panama Canal is just 64 kilometres long. It was built across the narrowest part of Central America.

ATLANTIC OCEAN

Grand Bahama I.
Great Abaco I.
Straits of Florida
Nassau
Andros I.
BAHAMAS
Tropic of Cancer

Gulf of Mexico

Havana
CUBA
Great Bahama Bank
Turks & Caicos Islands (to U.K.)

Yucatán Channel
Mérida
Isle of Pines
Holguín

Yucatán Peninsula
Cozumel I.
G r e a t e r
Santiago de Cuba
Windward Passage
HAITI
DOMINICAN REPUBLIC
Virgin Islands (to U.K./U.S.A.)

Bay of Campeche
Cayman Islands (to U.K.)
Port-au-Prince
San Juan
Anguilla (to U.K)

BELIZE
Belmopan
Kingston
JAMAICA
Santo Domingo
Puerto Rico (to U.S.A.)
ST. KITTS & NEVIS
ANTIGUA & BARBUDA
Montserrat (to U.K.)
Guadeloupe (to France)

A n t i l l e s

GUATEMALA
Chiapa R.
Gulf of Honduras
DOMINICA

HONDURAS
Guatemala City
R. Coco
C a r i b b e a n   S e a
Martinique (to France)

San Salvador
Tegucigalpa
ST. LUCIA
Bridgetown

EL SALVADOR
NICARAGUA
León
Aruba (to Netherlands)
ST. VINCENT & THE GRENADINES
BARBADOS

Managua
L. Nicaragua
L e s s e r   A n t i l l e s
GRENADA

Netherlands Antilles (to Netherlands)

TRINIDAD & TOBAGO
Port of Spain

COSTA RICA
San José
Panama Canal
Panama City
Gulf of Darien

Coronado Bay
PANAMA
Gulf of Panama
COLOMBIA
VENEZUELA

Gulf of Chiriquí

15

SOUTH AMERICA

The spectacular continent of South America contains some of Earth's most amazing places. In the north, the mighty River Amazon powers through the hot, wet rainforest on its journey to the Atlantic Ocean. Travelling south, tropical forests give way to the grassy lands of the Pampas and then to the cold, high Patagonian plateau. A long chain of mountains, called the Andes, towers above the Pacific coast.

Animals of the Amazon

Morpho butterfly

Toco toucan

Woolly spider monkey

Giant armadillo

Secrets in the Jungle

Amazonia covers more than six million square kilometres. It is the world's largest tropical rainforest. This gigantic jungle is home to more species than anywhere else on Earth.

Meeting of the Waters

The muddy, brown River Amazon joins the clear, dark River Negro near Manaus in Brazil. Like oil and water, these different waters do not mix well – a line of swirls marks the place where they meet.

Far to Fall

Angel Falls in Venezuela is the tallest waterfall on Earth. Water drops off a cliff and falls for 979 metres. This is 18 times higher than the Niagara Falls in North America!

Giant tortoises are only found on the volcanic Galapagos Islands.

Maracaibo　　Margarita I.　ATLANTIC

Gulf of Darien

Caracas

L. Maracaibo

VENEZUELA

Orinoco

Georgetown

Paramaribo

The Amazon carries more water to the sea than any other river. It hits the salty Atlantic with such force that it pushes a stream of fresh water 160 kilometres out into the ocean.

Medellín

Angel Falls

Cayenne

OCEAN

Bogotá

Guiana Highlands

French Guiana (to France)

Cali

COLOMBIA

R. Caquetá

R. Negro

Equator

Quito

ECUADOR

Belém

Fortaleza

Galapagos Islands (to Ecuador)

Guayaquil

R. Amazon

Manaus

Cape São Roque

R. Marañón

A m a z o n i a

B R A Z I L

Recife

PACIFIC

PERU

Andes

R. Madeira

R. Tapajós

R. Xingu

R. Araguaia

R. Tocantins

R. São Francisco

Brazilian Highlands

Salvador

The Atacama Desert is the driest place on Earth. Until 1971, there had been no rain here for 400 years.

Lima

R. Manoré

Plateau of Mato Grosso

Brasília

L. Titicaca

Altiplano

La Paz

BOLIVIA

R. Paraguay

Belo Horizonte

The Pampas is a vast area of grassy plains. It is bigger than Spain and Portugal put together.

L. Poopó

L. Salar de Uyuni

Rio de Janeiro

OCEAN

Atacama Desert

PARAGUAY

São Paulo　Tropic of Capricorn

Curitiba

Salt, No Pepper

Every year, summers are so hot high up on the Altiplano plain in Bolivia, that salty Lake Salar de Uyuni dries up. All that is left is a crust of salt that is six metres deep.

L. Salinas Grandes

Asunción

Pôrto Alegre

Córdoba

R. Paraná

Santa Fe

Mt. Aconcagua 6960m▲

Santiago

Pampas

URUGUAY

R. Salado

Montevideo

Buenos Aires

R. Plate

ARGENTINA

CHILE

R. Colorado

San Matías Gulf

Patagonia is a huge area of raised land.

Chiloé I.

N
W E
S

San Jorge Gulf

A strait is a narrow stretch of water.

Falkland Islands (to U.K.)

0　200　400　600　800　1000 km

0　200　400　600　miles

Paine Horns

Punta Arenas

Strait of Magellan

ATLANTIC OCEAN

Ice at Work

The Paine Horns in southern Chile are part of the Andes. These strange-shaped peaks were formed by volcanoes and then carved by ice.

Cape Horn

NORTHERN AFRICA

Almost all of Northern Africa lies north of the equator. The centre of this half of the African continent is filled by the Earth's largest and hottest desert – the Sahara. This sandy region stretches from the Atlantic Ocean to the Red Sea. The northwest edge of this huge, dry area rises up into the high, snowy Atlas Mountains. As you move towards the equator, the weather is wetter and hot desert changes into grassland and then to thick tropical rainforest.

Any place in the desert where water reaches the surface, such as Tamanrasset in Algeria, is known as an oasis.

M e d i t e r

Ceuta *(to Spain)*
Melilla *(to Spain)*
Tangier
Casablanca ■Rabat
Marrakesh

Algiers ■
Oran
Constantine
■Tunis
TUNISIA
Sfax
Tri

Al' Aziziyah

Wadi
Rua

MOROCCO
Atlas Mountains

ALGERIA

*S a h a r a
D e s e r t*

L

El Aaiún

**WESTERN
SAHARA**

●Fdérik

Tamanrasset Oasis
*Ahaggar
Mountains*

MAURITANIA
■Nouakchott

MALI
●Timbuktu

NIGER
Agadez

R. Senegal

R. Niger

S   *a*   *h*   *e*   *l*

CAPE VERDE

Dakar ■
GAMBIA
Banjul ■
SENEGAL

Bamako ■
R. Niger

Niamey

L
Ch

■Praia

Bissau ■
**GUINEA-
BISSAU**

GUINEA

Conakry ■
Freetown ■
SIERRA LEONE
Monrovia

Ouagadougou

BURKINA

**IVORY
COAST**

GHANA

BENIN
TOGO

N'Djamena

NIGERIA

R. Niger
■Abuja

Porto-Novo

*Adamawa
Highlands*

Yamoussoukro

LIBERIA

Abidjan
Accra
Lomé
Lagos

CAMEROON

Gulf of Guinea

Yaoundé

*The Sahel
is a strip of tropical
grassland that lies between
the dry Sahara and the
wet rainforests to the south.*

**EQUATORIAL
GUINEA**

GABON

CO

N
W E
S

0   200   400   600   800 km
0 100 200 300 400 500 miles

Tree-mendous Tropics
The trees in Cameroon stand 30 metres tall, their tops touching to form a thick canopy. Little sunlight gets through this leafy roof to reach the rainforest floor.

Sand Castles in the Air

The Sahara Desert spreads over about nine million square kilometres. Nearly one-quarter is covered in sand, the rest is rocky. In Libya, the hot sand is blown into dunes that can be taller than a 65-storey building!

The highest temperature recorded on Earth was at Al' Azīzīyah in Libya. It rose to 58°C.

Sahara's Survivors

Desert scorpion

Desert locust

Dung beetle

Common chameleon

No Soft Centre

The volcanic Ahaggar Mountains in southern Algeria form a massive island that rises high above the surrounding sand and rock.

The Nile is the Earth's longest river. It flows for 6,670 kilometres and brings water to dry, desert lands.

Benghazi, Gulf Sirte, Nile Delta, Port Said, Alexandria, Qattâra Depression, Cairo, Giza, R. Nile, LIBYA, EGYPT, Libyan Desert, Aswân, Tropic of Cancer, L. Nasser, Nubian Desert, Tibesti Mountains, CHAD, Wadi el Milk, R. Nile, Port Sudan, Red Sea, ERITREA, Omdurman, Khartoum, Asmara, SUDAN, Blue Nile, Danakil Depression, L. Tana, DJIBOUTI, Gulf of Aden, Djibouti, White Nile, Ethiopian Highlands, Hargeysa, Sarh, Sudd, Addis Ababa, ETHIOPIA, SOMALIA, R. Shebeli, CENTRAL AFRICAN REPUBLIC, L. Turkana, R. Juba, Bangui, ZAIRE, UGANDA, KENYA, INDIAN OCEAN, Mogadishu, Equator

The Sudd is a huge swamp. It covers 129,500 square kilometres – an area about the size of England.

Weird Water

You can't drink the water that bubbles out of the ground in the Danakil Depression in Ethiopia. It is full of a smelly, yellow substance called sulphur.

SOUTHERN AFRICA

The southern half of Africa is a jigsaw of different climates. Near the equator in the Congo Basin it is hot and wet. This weather is ideal for tropical rainforests. As you travel south, the climate gets drier and thick jungles give way to savanna – vast, open grasslands with scattered trees. Towards the southwest of Southern Africa, it is so dry that there are large, sandy deserts.

Thundering Down
The slow, sleepy River Zambezi tips over a high, wide ledge of rock at Victoria Falls. Local people call this waterfall 'The Smoke that Thunders' because it makes so much spray and noise.

Super Swamp
The River Okavango never reaches the sea. Instead, its waters empty into a vast area of flat land in Botswana to form a swampy delta.

Sea fog travels up to 20 kilometres inland each night and waters the few plants that manage to survive in the hot, sandy Namib Desert.

Table for a Giant
Table Mountain, which towers above Cape Town, has a flat top. When clouds roll over it, the 'table' looks as if it is covered by a tablecloth!

The climate and plants at the tip of Africa are similar to those found around the Mediterranean Sea.

Malabo
Bioko
CAMEROON
SAO TOME & PRINCIPE
São Tomé
EQUATORIAL GUINEA
Libreville
Port-Gentil   **GABON**
CENTRAL AFRICA REPUBLIC
R. Ubangi
R. Congo
Cong Basi
ZAIR
Brazzaville
Pointe-Noire
Cabinda
Kinshasa
Kananga
Mbuji-Ma
R. Kasai
Luanda
R. Cuanza
ANGOLA
Huambo
Cunene R.
R. Okavango
Cape Fria
Okavan Del
NAMIBIA
Namib Desert
Walvis Bay
Windhoek
BO
Kalaha Desert
R. Fish
SO
Orange R.
AFR
Cape Town
Table Mt.108
Cape of Good Hope

The Great Rift Valley is a long, wide dip in the ground which runs from Mozambique to Jordan in the Middle East.

SUDAN
ETHIOPIA
Uele
UGANDA
L. Turkana
KENYA
Kampala
Mt. Kirinyaga
5200m
Equator
RWANDA
L. Victoria
Nairobi
Kigali
BURUNDI
Bujumbura
Mt. Kilimanjaro
5895m
Great Rift Valley
TANZANIA
Mombasa
Dodoma
Zanzibar I.
L. Tanganyika
Dar es Salaam
L. Mweru
MALAWI
L. Nyasa
Cape Delgado
Lubumbashi
Moroni
Kitwe
Ndola
COMOROS
AMBIA
Lilongwe
Mayotte I.
(to France)
usaka
L. Cabora
R. Zambezi
Blantyre
Bassa
toria
L. Kariba
Harare
Chitungwiza
ZIMBABWE
Beira
Bulawayo
WANA
R. Limpopo
Gaborone
toria
Maputo
hannesburg
Mbabane
SWAZILAND
H
Bloemfontein
Maseru
SOTHO
Durban
A
Port Elizabeth
Drakensberg Mts.

MOZAMBIQUE
Mozambique Channel
Tropic of Capricorn

MADAGASCAR

SEYCHELLES
Victoria
Mahé I.
Amirante Islands

*Agalega Islands
(to Mauritius)*

*Tromelin I.
(to France)*

Antananarivo

Port Louis
MAURITIUS
Fianarantsoa
*Réunion I.
(to France)*

INDIAN OCEAN

Compass:
N
W — E
S

0 200 400 600 800 km
0 100 200 300 400 500 miles

Pastures New

Tropical grasslands are home to herds of zebra and wildebeest. When the grass dries out in the summer, these huge herds travel long distances across the savanna in search of fresh grass and water.

Most places near the equator are very hot, but Mount Kilimanjaro is so high that its top is covered in snow!

Wild Wanderers

Lion

Ostrich

Black rhinoceros

Odd One Out

Many unusual species, such as these spiny palm trees, have evolved on Madagascar because this island, and all its wildlife, split from the rest of Africa about 50 million years ago.

Giraffe

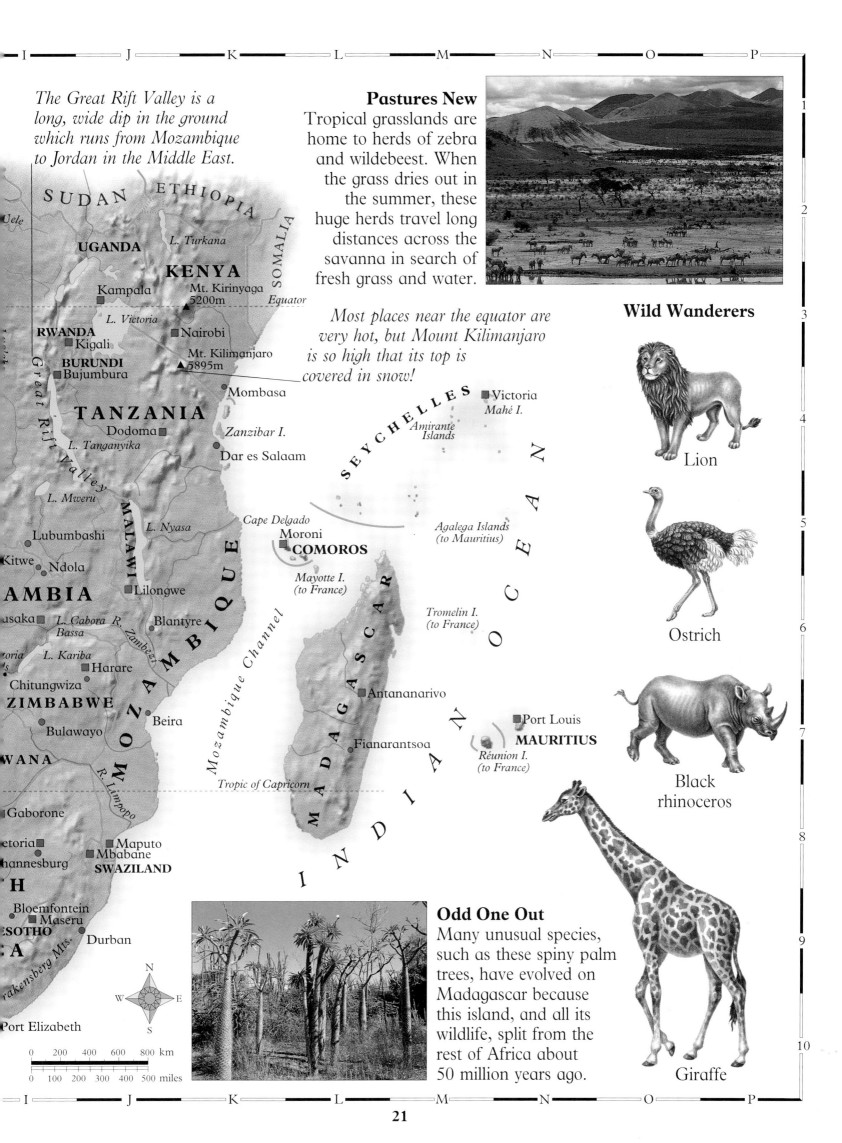

NORTHERN EUROPE

Norway and Sweden sit on a piece of land separated from most of Finland by the Gulf of Bothnia. These are countries with huge forests and spectacular lakes, with snow covering the mountains towards the north. The climate gets milder in Denmark and southern Sweden. The west coast of Norway is also mild because it is warmed by a current of water called the North Atlantic Drift, which travels across the ocean from North America.

Hot Below, Cold Above

Iceland is not as cold as it looks. Heat from the Earth's centre escapes, melting the edges of Iceland's great ice sheet, called Vatnajökull, to make chilly lakes.

Lights in the Sky

The skies in the extreme north are sometimes lit up by colourful, shimmering lights. This is called an aurora. It is caused by a stream of electrically charged particles that come from the sun.

Way, way out in the cold North Atlantic Ocean there are 18 volcanic islands called the Faeroes. Even farther still is the large island of Iceland.

A Scots pine tree grows by Lake Inari.

Green Giants

Aspen
(20 metres)

Silver birch
(30 metres)

Scots pine
(35 metres)

Norway spruce
(50 metres)

Lapping Waters

Lake Inari is a vast lake that lies in the north of Finland. It is so big that more than 3,000 tiny forested islands sit in its waters. In places it is deep enough to cover a 22-storey building.

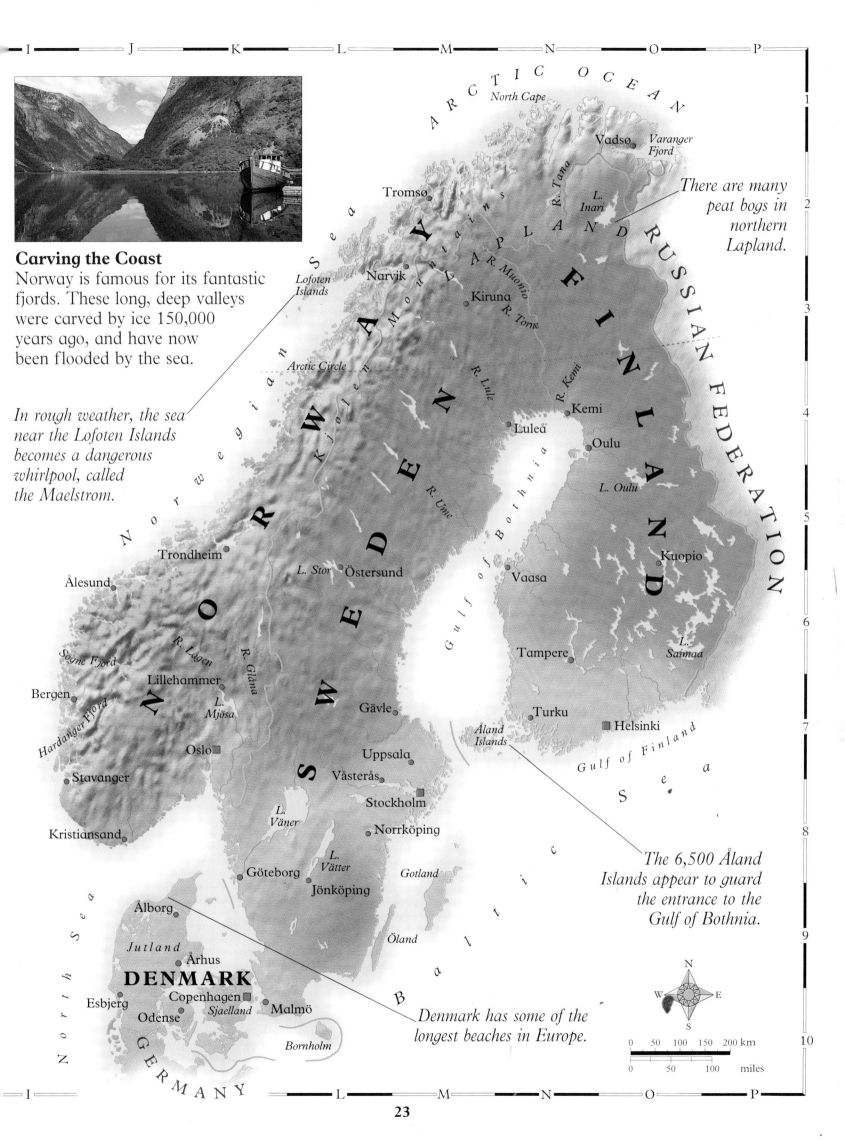

ARCTIC OCEAN

North Cape

Vadsø

Varanger Fjord

There are many peat bogs in northern Lapland.

Tromsø

R. Tana

L. Inari

RUSSIAN FEDERATION

Carving the Coast

Norway is famous for its fantastic fjords. These long, deep valleys were carved by ice 150,000 years ago, and have now been flooded by the sea.

In rough weather, the sea near the Lofoten Islands becomes a dangerous whirlpool, called the Maelstrom.

Lofoten Islands

Narvik

R. Muonio

Kiruna

R. Torne

Arctic Circle

R. Lule

R. Kemi

Kemi

Luleå

Oulu

L. Oulu

Trondheim

L. Stor

Östersund

Ålesund

Vaasa

Kuopio

R. Ume

Gulf of Bothnia

Sogne Fjord

R. Lågen

R. Glana

Lillehammer

Tampere

L. Saimaa

Bergen

Hardanger Fjord

L. Mjösa

Gävle

Turku

Helsinki

Oslo

Åland Islands

Gulf of Finland

Uppsala

Stavanger

Västerås

Kristiansand

Stockholm

The 6,500 Åland Islands appear to guard the entrance to the Gulf of Bothnia.

L. Väner

Norrköping

Göteborg

L. Vätter

Gotland

Jönköping

Ålborg

Öland

Jutland

Århus

DENMARK

Esbjerg

Copenhagen

Sjaelland

Malmö

Odense

Denmark has some of the longest beaches in Europe.

Bornholm

N

W E

S

GERMANY

NORWAY

SWEDEN

FINLAND

LAPLAND

Kjolen Mountains

Norwegian Sea

North Sea

Baltic Sea

0 50 100 150 200 km

0 50 100 miles

WESTERN EUROPE

The part of Europe that lies farthest away from Asia is known as Western Europe. The coasts that face the cool Atlantic Ocean are wet and windy. Inland, away from the sea, it is usually drier and less stormy. Generally, the farther south you travel in Western Europe, the hotter it becomes. By the time you reach the shores of the Mediterranean Sea, the summers are hot and dry.

Classic Columns
More than 60 million years ago, boiling hot lava slowly poured out of the ocean floor near Northern Ireland. The lava cooled into tall columns of rock, called the Giant's Causeway.

Into the Woods
The climate in the United Kingdom is temperate. This means that it is never too hot or too cold, and there is plenty of rain for beech and oak trees.

Woodland Wanderers

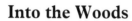

Pipistrelle bat

European stoat

European badger

Red fox

Strong Skittles
Although they are called the Ninepins, you could never bowl over these rugged rocks! They lie in northeast Spain amongst the Sierra de Loarre mountains.

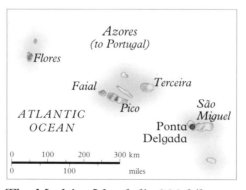

The Madeira Islands lie 900 kilometres southwest of Portugal. The Azores are more remote, they are one-third of the way to North America.

The Canary Islands lie 1,400 kilometres off the southwest coast of Spain.

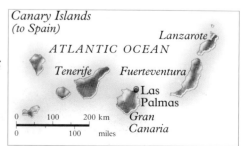

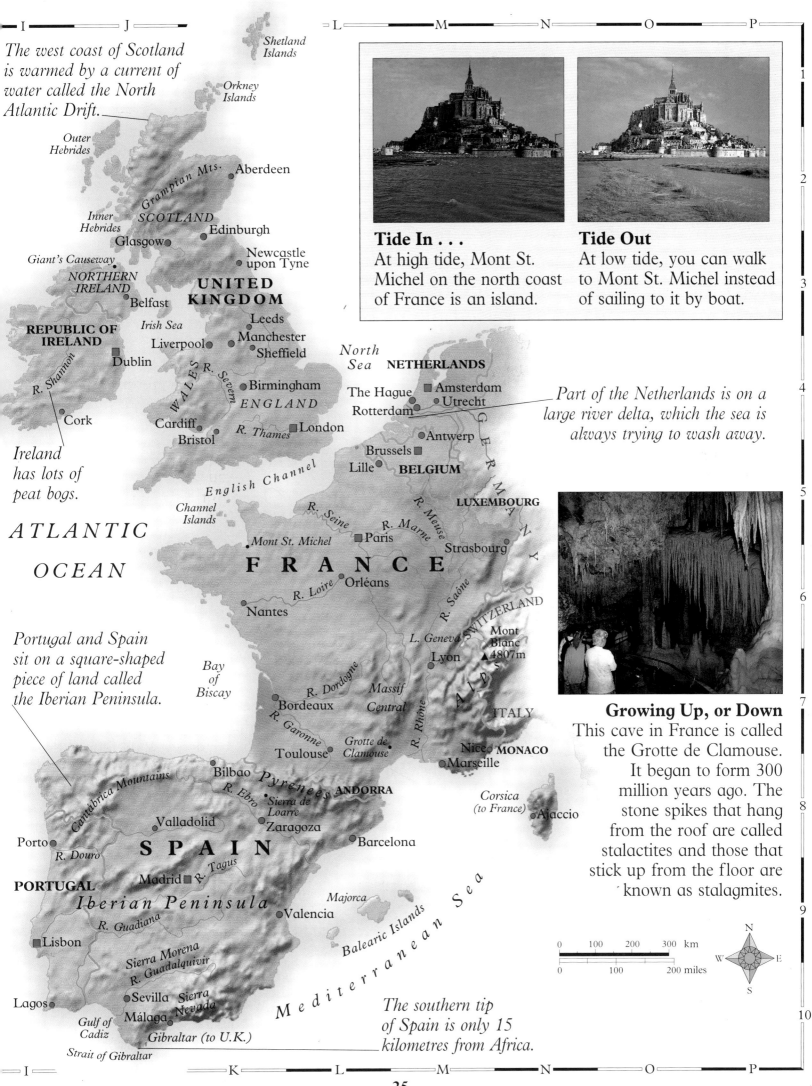

The west coast of Scotland is warmed by a current of water called the North Atlantic Drift.

Shetland Islands

Orkney Islands

Outer Hebrides

Grampian Mts. • Aberdeen

Inner Hebrides

SCOTLAND
Glasgow • Edinburgh
• Newcastle upon Tyne

Giant's Causeway

NORTHERN IRELAND
• Belfast

UNITED KINGDOM

REPUBLIC OF IRELAND
Irish Sea
Leeds •
Liverpool • • Manchester
• Sheffield

Dublin ■

R. Shannon

Cork •

Ireland has lots of peat bogs.

WALES
R. Severn
• Birmingham
ENGLAND
Cardiff •
Bristol •
R. Thames • London

North Sea

NETHERLANDS
The Hague ■ Amsterdam
Rotterdam • Utrecht

Part of the Netherlands is on a large river delta, which the sea is always trying to wash away.

• Antwerp
Brussels ■
Lille • BELGIUM

GERMANY

ATLANTIC OCEAN

English Channel

Channel Islands

Mont St. Michel •

R. Seine
Paris ■

R. Marne

R. Meuse

LUXEMBOURG

F R A N C E

Strasbourg •

R. Loire
• Orléans

Nantes •

R. Saône

SWITZERLAND

L. Geneva
Lyon •

Mont Blanc
▲4807m

A L P S

Portugal and Spain sit on a square-shaped piece of land called the Iberian Peninsula.

Bay of Biscay

R. Dordogne

Massif Central

Bordeaux •

R. Garonne

R. Rhône

Grotte de Clamouse •
Toulouse •

ITALY

Nice • MONACO
• Marseille

Bilbao •
Pyrenees ANDORRA

Corsica (to France)
• Ajaccio

Cantábrica Mountains

R. Ebro
Sierra de Loarre

Valladolid •
Zaragoza •

• Barcelona

Porto •
R. Douro

S P A I N

PORTUGAL
Madrid ■ R. Tagus

Iberian Peninsula
R. Guadiana
• Valencia

Majorca

Balearic Islands

Lisbon ■

Sierra Morena
R. Guadalquivir

Mediterranean Sea

Lagos •

Sevilla • Sierra Nevada
Málaga •
Gibraltar (to U.K.)

Gulf of Cadiz

Strait of Gibraltar

The southern tip of Spain is only 15 kilometres from Africa.

Tide In . . .
At high tide, Mont St. Michel on the north coast of France is an island.

Tide Out
At low tide, you can walk to Mont St. Michel instead of sailing to it by boat.

Growing Up, or Down
This cave in France is called the Grotte de Clamouse. It began to form 300 million years ago. The stone spikes that hang from the roof are called stalactites and those that stick up from the floor are known as stalagmites.

0   100   200   300 km
0   100   200 miles

N
W   E
S

CENTRAL EUROPE

The land that stretches from the Baltic Sea to the Mediterranean Sea is known as Central Europe. Halfway down, it is cut in two by a range of snow-covered mountains called the Alps. The area to the north of this divide includes the cool, forested plains of Germany and Poland. Italy, to the south, is a long peninsula of land, surrounded by warm seas, such as the Mediterranean.

Road of Water

It is possible for ships to sail all the way up the River Rhine, through Germany, to Switzerland. The river runs through many green valleys on its long journey of 1,320 kilometres.

Alpine Plants

Alpine aster

King of the Alps

The Hills are Alive

During the spring, these slopes are a mass of colourful alpine flowers. They have survived the cold winter frosts by being covered by a thick blanket of snow.

Slipping Away

Some of the snow on top of the Swiss Alps freezes into rivers of ice, called glaciers. Each glacier slowly slips down the mountain. When they reach the warm lower slopes, they melt into streams.

Mediterranean Plants

Wild sage

Poppy

Summer Survivors

The poppies growing on this coast in southern Italy can live without much water. Plants that grow around the Mediterranean Sea have to survive hot, dry summers.

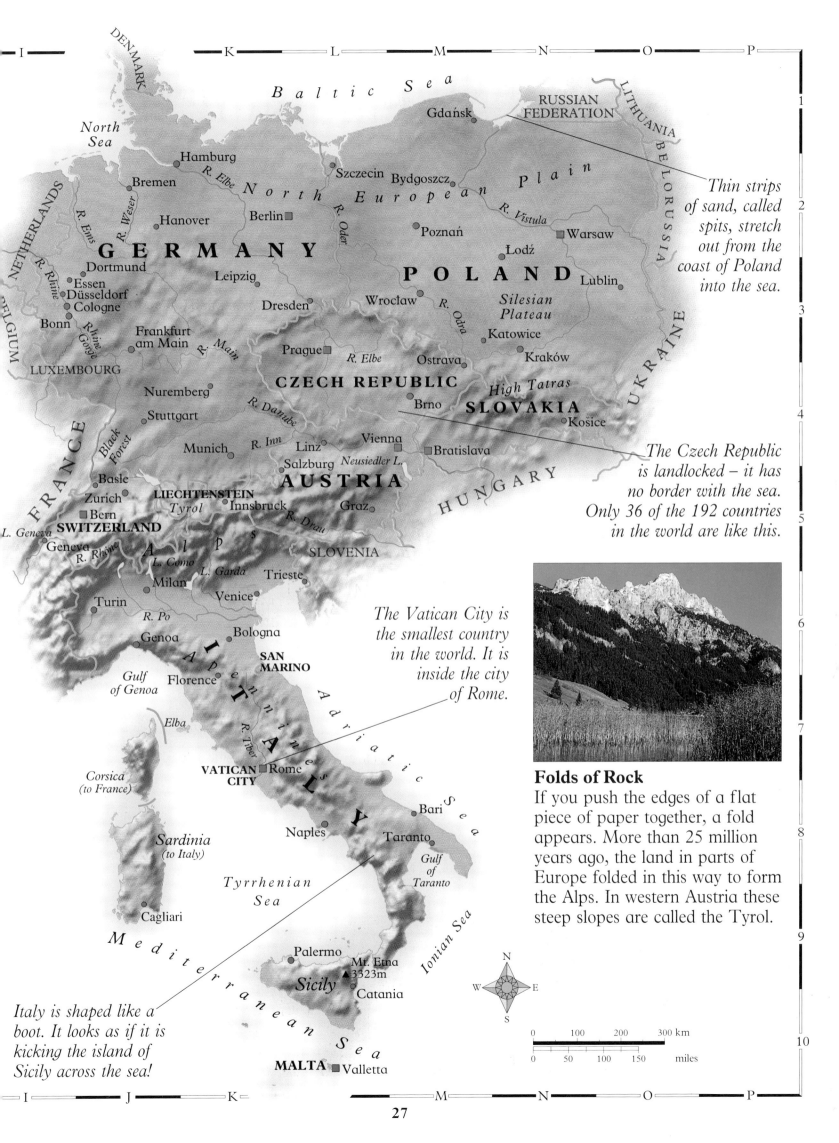

Baltic Sea

DENMARK

North Sea

Gdańsk

RUSSIAN FEDERATION

LITHUANIA

BELORUSSIA

Hamburg

Bremen

Szczecin Bydgoszcz

North   *European*   *Plain*

R. Elbe

Berlin

Hanover

R. Ems

R. Weser

Poznań

Warsaw

R. Vistula

GERMANY

Łodz

P O L A N D

NETHERLANDS

Dortmund

Leipzig

Lublin

Essen

Düsseldorf

Cologne

R. Rhine

Wrocław

Dresden

R. Oder

R. Odra

Silesian Plateau

UKRAINE

Bonn

Frankfurt am Main

Rhine Gorge

Katowice

BELGIUM

LUXEMBOURG

R. Main

Prague

R. Elbe

Ostrava

Kraków

Nuremberg

CZECH REPUBLIC

High Tatras

Brno **SLOVAKIA**

Stuttgart

R. Danube

Košice

FRANCE

Black Forest

Munich

R. Inn

Linz

Vienna

Bratislava

Salzburg

Neusiedler L.

Basle

LIECHTENSTEIN

Innsbruck

AUSTRIA

Graz

H U N G A R Y

Zurich

Tyrol

Bern

R. Drau

SWITZERLAND

L. Geneva

A   l   p   s

SLOVENIA

Geneva

R. Rhône

L. Como

L. Garda

Trieste

Milan

Venice

Turin

R. Po

Bologna

Genoa

SAN MARINO

Gulf of Genoa

Florence

A   p   e   n   n   i   n   e   s

Adriatic Sea

Elba

R. Tiber

VATICAN CITY Rome

Corsica (to France)

I T A L Y

Bari

Naples

Taranto

Sardinia (to Italy)

Gulf of Taranto

Tyrrhenian Sea

Cagliari

Ionian Sea

M e d i t e r r a n e a n

Palermo

Mt. Etna ▲ 3323m

Sicily

Catania

M a l t a S e a

MALTA Valletta

Thin strips of sand, called spits, stretch out from the coast of Poland into the sea.

The Czech Republic is landlocked – it has no border with the sea. Only 36 of the 192 countries in the world are like this.

The Vatican City is the smallest country in the world. It is inside the city of Rome.

Folds of Rock

If you push the edges of a flat piece of paper together, a fold appears. More than 25 million years ago, the land in parts of Europe folded in this way to form the Alps. In western Austria these steep slopes are called the Tyrol.

Italy is shaped like a boot. It looks as if it is kicking the island of Sicily across the sea!

N
W   E
S

| | 0 | 100 | 200 | 300 km |
| 0 | 50 | 100 | 150 | miles |

EASTERN EUROPE

The eastern side of Europe is dotted with many large lakes and small seas. It is a land of contrasts. The northern half is cold, fairly flat and mostly taken up by one enormous country, the Russian Federation. The southern half of Eastern Europe is quite different. It is warmer, more mountainous and split into many smaller countries, such as Moldavia and Macedonia. This southern region is also much more likely to be shaken by earthquakes.

When it freezes in winter, you can walk on the White Sea.

Nice Spots
The Adriatic Sea is very slowly flooding the southwest corner of Eastern Europe. Gradually, low land disappears under the waves, leaving only the tops of hills above water level. This type of coast is called a dalmatian coast.

Many rare wetland birds nest amongst the reeds and rushes of the Pripet Marshes.

Worn Out
Water can carve through rock! A river on the island of Crete has cut out the Samaria Gorge. This deep valley twists and turns its way through the land for 18 kilometres.

Greece has so many inlets along its coastline that no place is more than 100 kilometres from the sea.

N
W E
S

| 0 | 200 | 400 | 600 km |

| 0 | 100 | 200 | 300 | miles |

Feathered Friends

Novaya Zemlya

I C   O C E A N

Kara Sea

Vaygach I.

Barents Sea

Kolguyev I.

Kola Poninsula

White Sea

The 2,000-kilometre-long Ural Mountains separate Europe from Asia. They also split the Russian Federation, the world's largest country, in two.

Arctic Circle

Arkhangel'sk

R. Pechora

Northern Dvina R.

Ural Mountains

Plain

R U S S I A N
F E D E R A T I O N

Hoopoe

Eurasian sparrowhawk

Great eagle owl

Rybinsk Reservoir

Nizhniy Novgorod

R. Kama

Moscow

Kuybyshev Reservoir

Samara

R. Volga

R. Don

K A Z A K H S T A N

R. Volga

Snow Down

The Carpathian Mountains are capped with snow. If this layer of snow suddenly slips, it hurtles down the slope, starting an avalanche.

The Caspian Sea is the largest lake on Earth. It is so big that it is called a sea.

Caspian Sea

Mt. El'brus
▲ 5462m

Caucasus Mountains

GEORGIA □ Tbilisi

AZERBAIJAN

ARMENIA

Purple heron

n the Black Sea, a 90-metre ayer of fresh water floats n the salty water.

View of a Valley

A valley is a strip of lower land surrounded by higher land. Many valleys, like the grassy dips in the Caucasus Mountains, are formed by glaciers.

THE MIDDLE EAST

The lands that lie where Africa, Europe and Asia meet are known as the Middle East. Almost all the southern half of this region is covered by sand and rocks. Here there are vast, hot, dry deserts – places where few plants survive. Many of the mountains and plateaus to the north are just as dry. It is only when you travel towards the shores of the Mediterranean Sea that there is more rain.

White Wonderland
At Pamukkale, in Turkey, a warm stream of water and minerals bubbles out of the ground. The minerals left behind by the water have formed a stairway of white, stone steps.

Salty Sea
The Dead Sea, which lies between Israel and Jordan, is the lowest place on Earth. It is nearly 400 metres lower than the surface of the Mediterranean Sea. It is also the saltiest area of water on Earth. The water is so salty that no fish can survive here.

Stones cover the desert floor.

Desert Dwellers

Arabian oryx   Egyptian vulture   Camel

Stony Heart
Much of central Iran is a cold, hilly desert. The strong winds have blown away most of the sand leaving bare, stony areas.

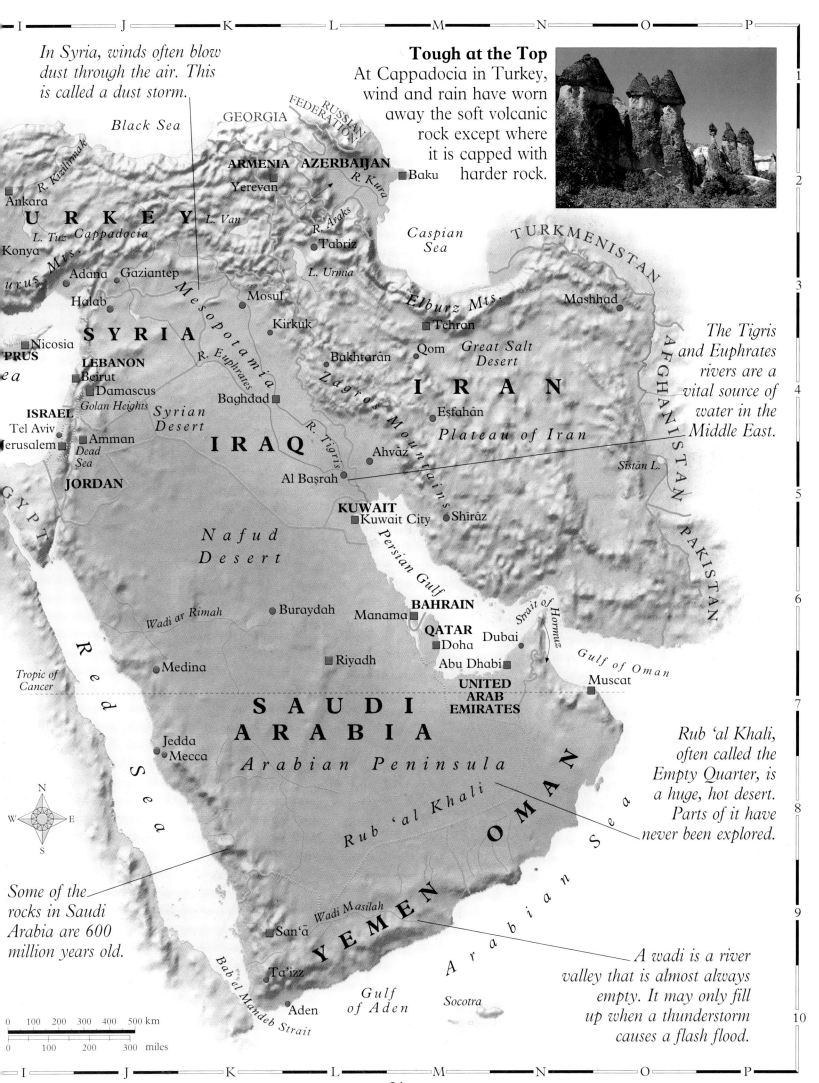

I J K L M N O P

1 2 3 4 5 6 7 8 9 10

In Syria, winds often blow dust through the air. This is called a dust storm.

Tough at the Top
At Cappadocia in Turkey, wind and rain have worn away the soft volcanic rock except where it is capped with harder rock.

Black Sea

GEORGIA
RUSSIAN FEDERATION

ARMENIA **AZERBAIJAN**
Yerevan
Baku
R. Kura

T U R K E Y
Ankara
R. Kızılırmak
L. Tuz
Cappadocia
Konya
L. Van
R. Araks
Caspian Sea

Adana
Gaziantep
Tabriz
L. Urmia

Halab
Mosul

S Y R I A
Kirkuk
Mashhad

Nicosia
Mesopotamia
R. Euphrates

PRUS
Sea
LEBANON
Beirut
Damascus
Golan Heights
Baghdad

I R A N
Tehran
Qom
Great Salt Desert

Bakhtaran
Eşfahān
Plateau of Iran

Elburz Mts.

The Tigris and Euphrates rivers are a vital source of water in the Middle East.

ISRAEL
Tel Aviv
Jerusalem
Amman
Dead Sea
Syrian Desert

I R A Q
R. Tigris
Ahvaz
Al Başrah

JORDAN
Sistān L.

EGYPT
KUWAIT
Kuwait City
Shirāz
Persian Gulf

Nafud Desert

Zagros Mountains

AFGHANISTAN PAKISTAN

TURKMENISTAN

Wadi ar Rimah
Buraydah
Manama
BAHRAIN
Strait of Hormuz

QATAR
Doha
Dubai
Gulf of Oman

Medina
Riyadh
Abu Dhabi
Muscat

Tropic of Cancer
UNITED ARAB EMIRATES

S A U D I
A R A B I A
Arabian Peninsula

O M A N

*Rub 'al Khali,
often called the
Empty Quarter, is
a huge, hot desert.
Parts of it have
never been explored.*

Jedda
Mecca

Rub 'al Khali

R e d   S e a

A r a b i a n   S e a

N
W   E
S

Some of the rocks in Saudi Arabia are 600 million years old.

Y E M E N

Wadi Masilah
San'a

A wadi is a river valley that is almost always empty. It may only fill up when a thunderstorm causes a flash flood.

Ta'izz
Gulf of Aden
Socotra
Aden
Bab el Mandeb Strait

0 100 200 300 400 500 km
0 100 200 300 miles

NORTH & CENTRAL ASIA

The world's largest forest is known as the taiga. It covers most of the cold, flat Siberian lands that stretch from the Ural Mountains to the Bering Sea. Few trees grow north of Siberia as they are unable to push their roots into the frozen ground. These freezing plains of the north are called the tundra. To the south of Siberia there are cold deserts, such as the Gobi, and huge grasslands, or steppes.

Severnaya Zemlya

Kara Sea

Yamal Peninsula

R. Yenisey

Central Siberia Plateau

Ural Mountains

R. Ob'

West Siberian Plain

R U S S I A N   F E D

R. Irtysh

R. Ob'

R. Angara

Yekaterinburg

Chelyabinsk

Omsk

Tomsk

Krasnoyarsk

Novosibirsk

Kustanai

Irk

Ural'sk

Aktyubinsk

Karaganda

Uliastay

Kirghiz Steppe

Altai Mountains

M O N

KAZAKHSTAN

L. Balkhash

Aral Sea

Alma-Ata

Caspian Sea

Bishkek

L. Issyk-Kul'

Gobi Des

UZBEKISTAN

KYRGYZSTAN

Tashkent

Osh

C

Samarkand

TURKMENISTAN

TAJIKISTAN

Ashgabat

Dushanbe

Hindu Kush

IRAN

Herāt

Kabul

Khyber Pass

AFGHANISTAN

Qandahār

No Way Out
Rain rarely falls on the dry Hindu Kush mountains in Afghanistan, so this lake is a glittering prize. It is here because rocks have formed a dam across a river.

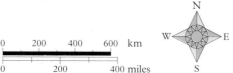

0	200	400	600 km
0	200	400 miles	

N
W E
S

Step by Step
There are many large plains in Mongolia. They are part of the enormous grasslands, called steppes, that curve across Central Asia.

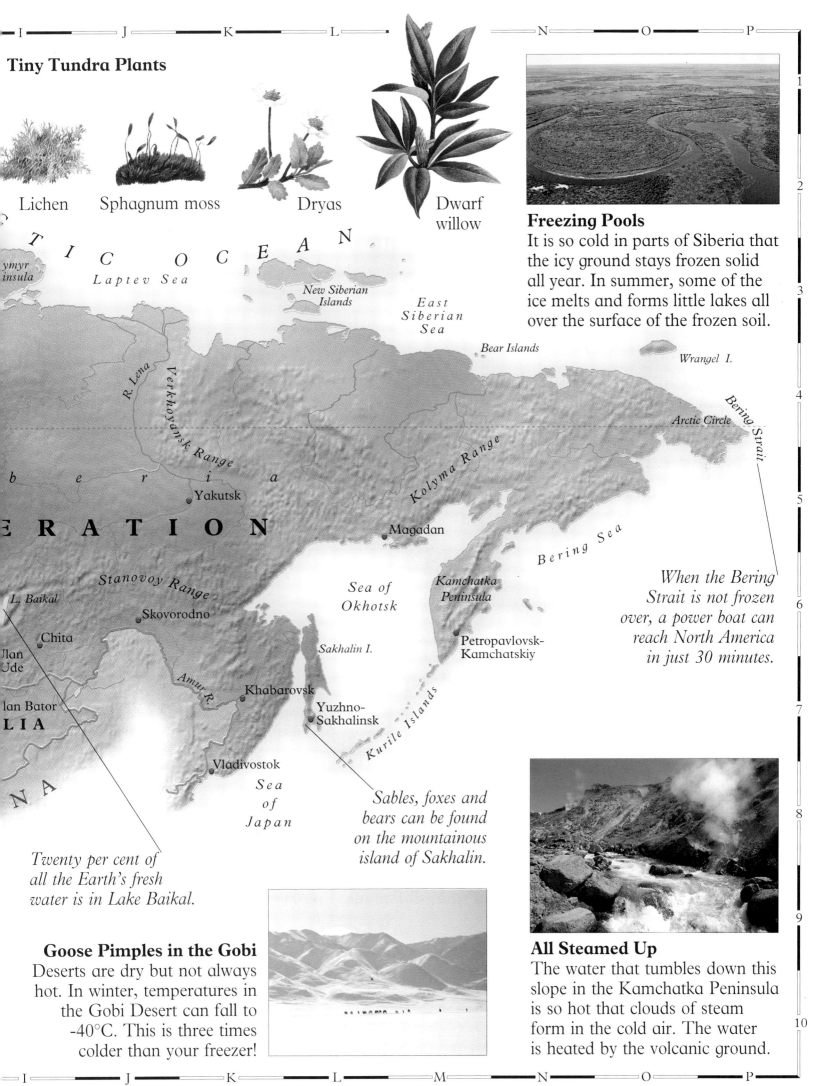

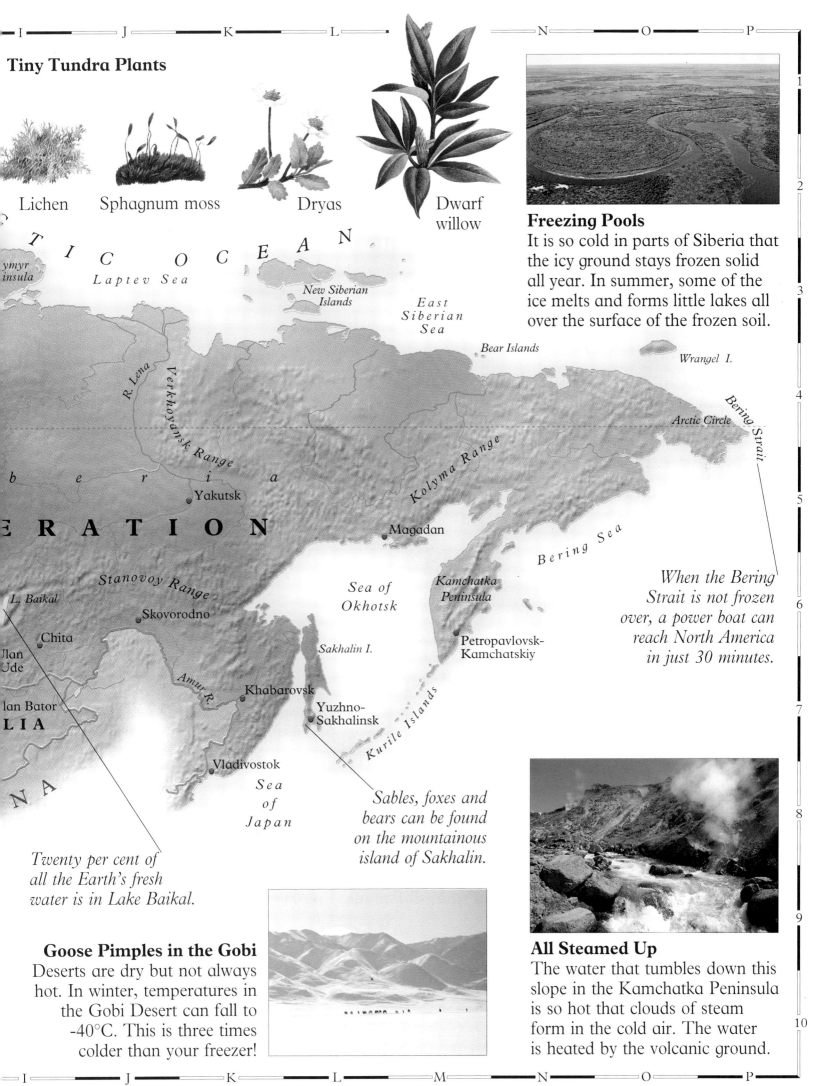

Tiny Tundra Plants

Lichen

Sphagnum moss

Dryas

Dwarf willow

Freezing Pools
It is so cold in parts of Siberia that the icy ground stays frozen solid all year. In summer, some of the ice melts and forms little lakes all over the surface of the frozen soil.

When the Bering Strait is not frozen over, a power boat can reach North America in just 30 minutes.

Sables, foxes and bears can be found on the mountainous island of Sakhalin.

Twenty per cent of all the Earth's fresh water is in Lake Baikal.

Goose Pimples in the Gobi
Deserts are dry but not always hot. In winter, temperatures in the Gobi Desert can fall to -40°C. This is three times colder than your freezer!

All Steamed Up
The water that tumbles down this slope in the Kamchatka Peninsula is so hot that clouds of steam form in the cold air. The water is heated by the volcanic ground.

Map labels:

ARCTIC OCEAN

Laptev Sea

ymyr insula

New Siberian Islands

East Siberian Sea

Bear Islands

Wrangel I.

R. Lena

Verkhoyansk Range

Kolyma Range

Arctic Circle

Bering Strait

b e r i a

Yakutsk

FEDERATION

Magadan

Bering Sea

Stanovoy Range

L. Baikal

Skovorodno

Chita

Ulan Ude

Ulan Bator

MONGOLIA

Amur R.

Khabarovsk

Sea of Okhotsk

Sakhalin I.

Kamchatka Peninsula

Petropavlovsk-Kamchatskiy

Sea of Japan

Kurile Islands

Yuzhno-Sakhalinsk

Vladivostok

CHINA

THE INDIAN SUBCONTINENT

The Himalayas are the Earth's highest mountain range. They form a vast wall of rock that splits up Asia. The triangular-shaped area to the south of this natural barrier is the Indian Subcontinent. This is a region of dramatically different climates, from the cold mountains of the north to the hot deserts of the west. Each summer heavy rains fall in the eastern and southern parts, blown in by the strong monsoon winds.

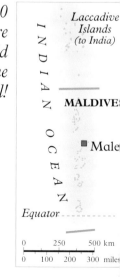

AFGHANISTAN
IRAN
Tobakakar
Quetta
PAKI
Hyderabad
Karachi
R. Indus
Gulf of K

Sand and rocks cover the Thar Desert. There is usually only half a metre of rain a year in this hot, dry place.

The Highest Place on Earth
Everest is the highest mountain in the world. The local people have a name for Everest which means 'Mountain So High That No Bird Can Fly Over It'.

Passing Over
You don't need to be a mountaineer to cross the mountains that divide Pakistan and Afghanistan. Instead, you can walk 50 kilometres through the long, narrow Khyber Pass.

There are about 2,000 Maldive Islands. They are all very flat – you would be almost as tall as the highest hill!

Laccadive Islands (to India)

INDIAN OCEAN

MALDIVE

■ Male

Equator

0   250   500 km
0 100 200 300 miles

Indian Animal Parade

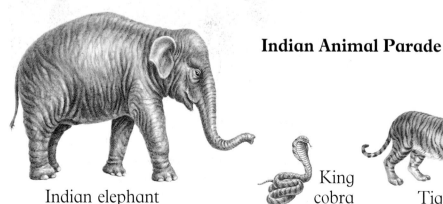

Indian elephant   King cobra   Tiger   Peacock

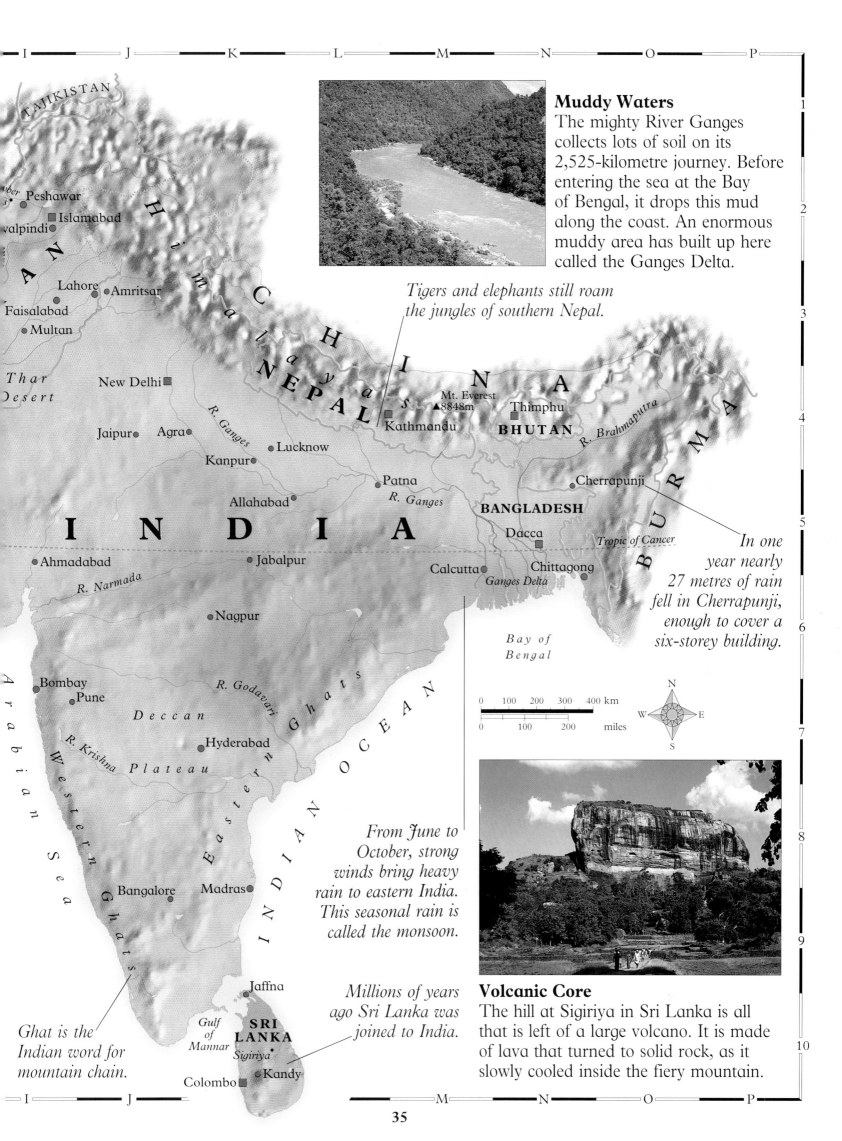

Muddy Waters
The mighty River Ganges collects lots of soil on its 2,525-kilometre journey. Before entering the sea at the Bay of Bengal, it drops this mud along the coast. An enormous muddy area has built up here called the Ganges Delta.

Tigers and elephants still roam the jungles of southern Nepal.

In one year nearly 27 metres of rain fell in Cherrapunji, enough to cover a six-storey building.

From June to October, strong winds bring heavy rain to eastern India. This seasonal rain is called the monsoon.

Millions of years ago Sri Lanka was joined to India.

Ghat is the Indian word for mountain chain.

Volcanic Core
The hill at Sigiriya in Sri Lanka is all that is left of a large volcano. It is made of lava that turned to solid rock, as it slowly cooled inside the fiery mountain.

TAJIKISTAN
Peshawar
Islamabad
valpindi
Lahore · Amritsar
Faisalabad
Multan
Thar Desert
New Delhi
Jaipur · Agra
Kanpur · Lucknow
Allahabad
Ahmadabad
R. Narmada
Jabalpur
Nagpur
Bombay
Pune
Deccan
R. Godavari
R. Krishna
Plateau
Hyderabad
Bangalore · Madras
HIMALAYA
Himalaya
NEPAL
Kathmandu
Mt. Everest ▲8848m
BHUTAN
Thimphu
R. Brahmaputra
CHINA
BURMA
Patna
R. Ganges
R. Ganges
Cherrapunji
BANGLADESH
Dacca
Calcutta
Chittagong
Ganges Delta
Tropic of Cancer
Bay of Bengal
Western Ghats
Eastern Ghats
INDIA
INDIAN OCEAN
Arabian Sea
Jaffna
Gulf of Mannar
SRI LANKA
Sigiriya
Colombo · Kandy

0 100 200 300 400 km
0 100 200 miles

N
W E
S

EAST ASIA

China takes up most of East Asia. The cold deserts and mountains in the west of this enormous country are some of Earth's most remote places. Between this empty region and the eastern coastline there are wetter, flat, grassy plains. Farther east, the Korean Peninsula stretches out towards the islands of Japan.

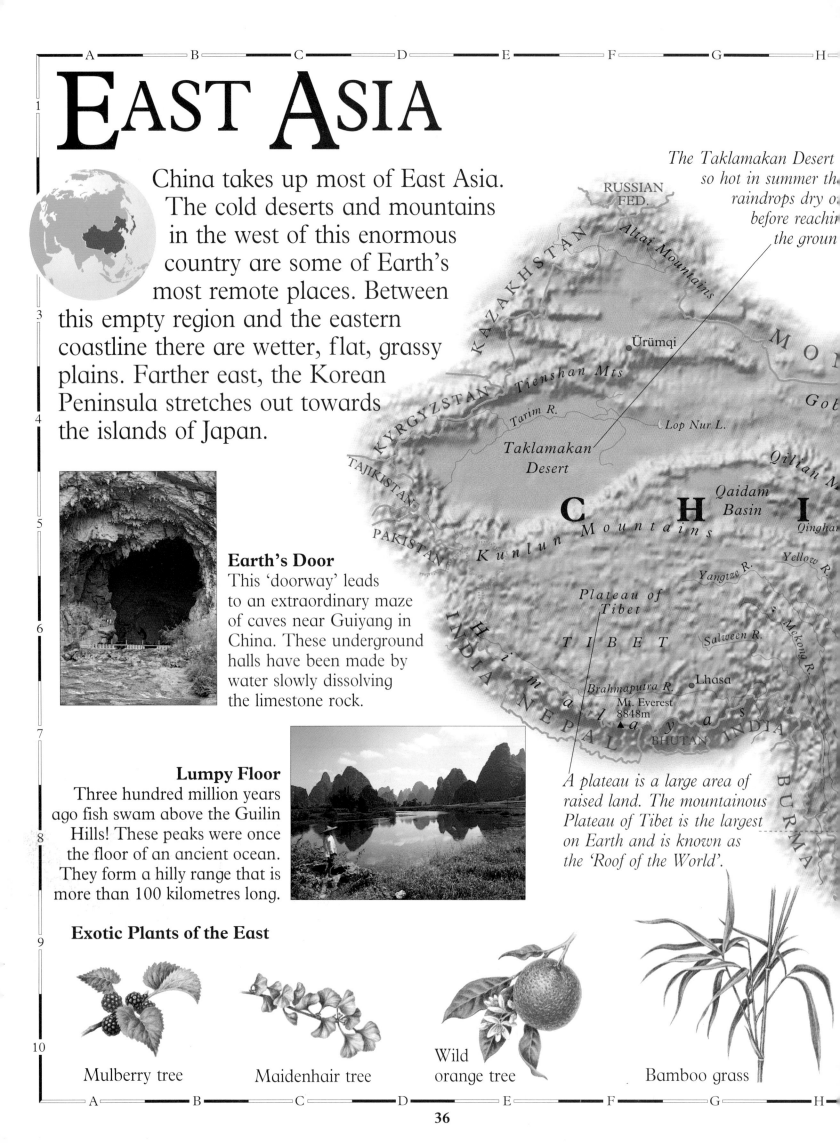

The Taklamakan Desert so hot in summer th raindrops dry o before reachin the groun

RUSSIAN FED.

Altai Mountains

KAZAKHSTAN

Ürümqi

KYRGYZSTAN

Tienshan Mts

Tarim R.

Lop Nur L.

Taklamakan Desert

TAJIKISTAN

PAKISTAN

Kunlun Mountains

Qaidam Basin

C H I

Qinghai

Qilian M

Yellow R.

Yangtze R.

Plateau of Tibet

T I B E T

Salween R.

Mekong R.

INDIA

Himalaya

Brahmaputra R.

Lhasa

Mt. Everest 8848m

NEPAL

BHUTAN

INDIA

BURMA

Go
M O
Go

Earth's Door
This 'doorway' leads to an extraordinary maze of caves near Guiyang in China. These underground halls have been made by water slowly dissolving the limestone rock.

Lumpy Floor
Three hundred million years ago fish swam above the Guilin Hills! These peaks were once the floor of an ancient ocean. They form a hilly range that is more than 100 kilometres long.

A plateau is a large area of raised land. The mountainous Plateau of Tibet is the largest on Earth and is known as the 'Roof of the World'.

Exotic Plants of the East

Mulberry tree

Maidenhair tree

Wild orange tree

Bamboo grass

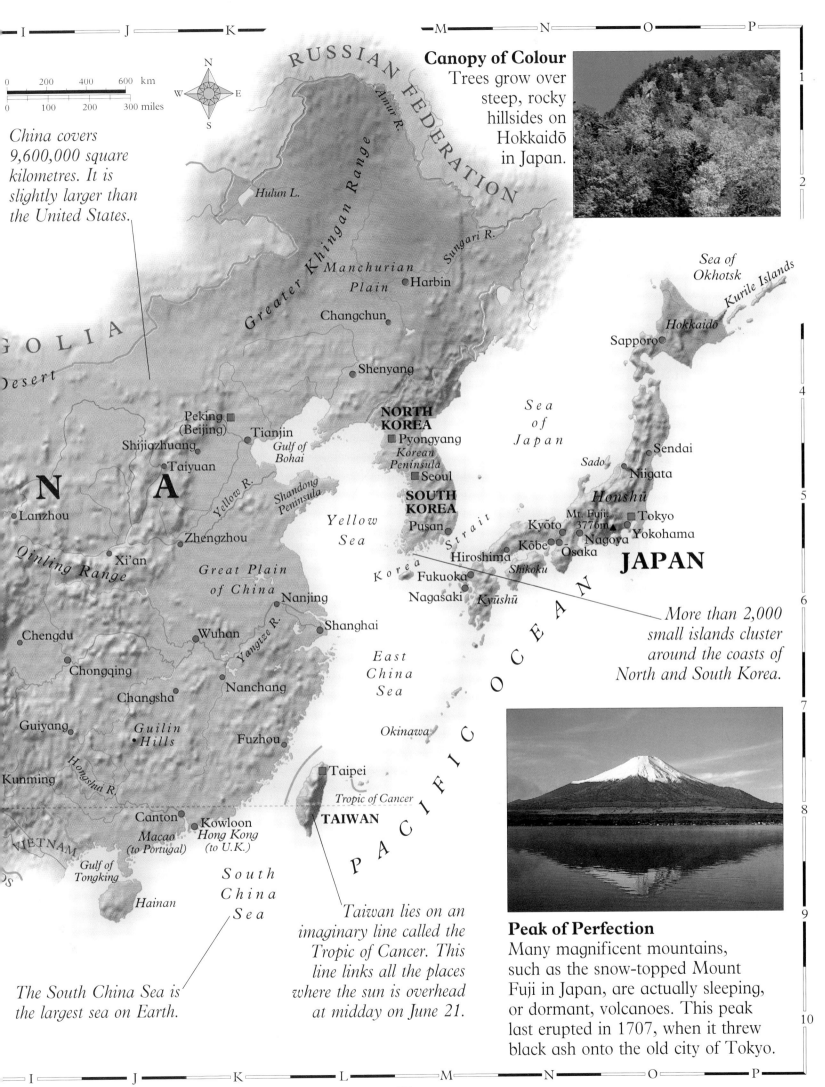

Canopy of Colour
Trees grow over steep, rocky hillsides on Hokkaidō in Japan.

China covers 9,600,000 square kilometres. It is slightly larger than the United States.

RUSSIAN FEDERATION

Amur R.

Greater Khingan Range

Hulun L.

Sea of Okhotsk

Kurile Islands

Manchurian Plain ●Harbin

Changchun

Hokkaidō

●Sapporo

GOLIA

Desert

Shenyang

Sungari R.

NORTH KOREA
■Pyongyang

Sea of Japan

Sado

●Sendai

Peking (Beijing)■
Tianjin●
Shijiazhuang●

Korean Peninsula

■Seoul

●Niigata

Honshū

N

Taiyuan●

Gulf of Bohai

SOUTH KOREA

Yellow R.

Shandong Peninsula

Kyoto● Mt. Fuji 3776m▲ ■Tokyo
●Yokohama

●Lanzhou

Zhengzhou●

Yellow Sea

Pusan●

Korea Strait

Kōbe●● Nagoya
Ōsaka●

JAPAN

Qinling Range

Xi'an●

Hiroshima●

Shikoku

Great Plain of China

Nanjing●

Fukuoka●

Chengdu●

Wuhan●

Yangtze R.

●Shanghai

Nagasaki●

Kyūshū

More than 2,000 small islands cluster around the coasts of North and South Korea.

Chongqing●

Nanchang●

East China Sea

Changsha●

Guiyang●

Guilin Hills

Fuzhou●

Okinawa

Honghui R.

Kunming●

Canton●

Macao (to Portugal)

Kowloon●
Hong Kong (to U.K.)

Tropic of Cancer

■Taipei

TAIWAN

VIETNAM

Gulf of Tongking

Hainan

South China Sea

Taiwan lies on an imaginary line called the Tropic of Cancer. This line links all the places where the sun is overhead at midday on June 21.

P A C I F I C   O C E A N

The South China Sea is the largest sea on Earth.

Peak of Perfection
Many magnificent mountains, such as the snow-topped Mount Fuji in Japan, are actually sleeping, or dormant, volcanoes. This peak last erupted in 1707, when it threw black ash onto the old city of Tokyo.

N
W   E
S

0   200   400   600 km
0   100   200   300 miles

SOUTHEAST ASIA

The islands in Southeast Asia form a chain that is about the same length as the distance across the United States. Cutting straight through the heart of this region there is an imaginary line called the Equator. Like most of the lands that lie on this line, Southeast Asia is hot all year round. The warm, moist air forms rainclouds, and there are many thunderstorms. Tropical rainforests grow in this hot, humid climate.

Powerful winds, called typhoons, crash into the coast of Vietnam.

INDIA

CHINA

BANGLADESH

BURMA

Mandalay

Irrawaddy R.

Salween R.

Red R.

LAOS

Hanoi

Hai Phong

Gulf of Tongking

Tropic of Cancer

Louang Phrabang

Bay of Bengal

Chiang Mai

R. Ping

Vientiane

Mekong R.

Pegu

Rangoon

Moulmein

VIETNAM

Da Na

THAILAND

Andaman Islands (to India)

Bangkok

CAMBODIA

L. Tônlé

Bâtdâmbâng

Port Blair

Andaman Sea

Gulf of Thailand

Phnom Penh

Isthmus of Kra

Ho Chi Minh City

Mekong Delta

Kakana

Malay Peninsula

Nakhon Si Thammarat

Phuket I.

Ko Phi Phi I.

Nicobar Islands (to India)

INDIAN

Pinang

MALAY

Strait of Malacca

Medan

Sumatra

Kuala Lumpur

Kuching

SINGAPORE

One of Many
Ko Phi Phi Island lies off Thailand's coast. It is one of more than 20,000 islands that are packed into this region. Many of them were formed by volcanoes.

Padang

Pontianak

Bangka I.

Palembang

I **N**

OCEAN

Java

Colourful Mystery
Brightly coloured lakes sit inside an extinct volcano on Flores Island. Nobody knows why, but sometimes the lakes suddenly change colour. In the past, the waters have looked blue, rusty-brown and black.

Jakarta

Krakatau I.

Semaran

Bandung

Java

In 1883, the island of Krakatau was torn apart by one of the world's largest volcanic explosions.

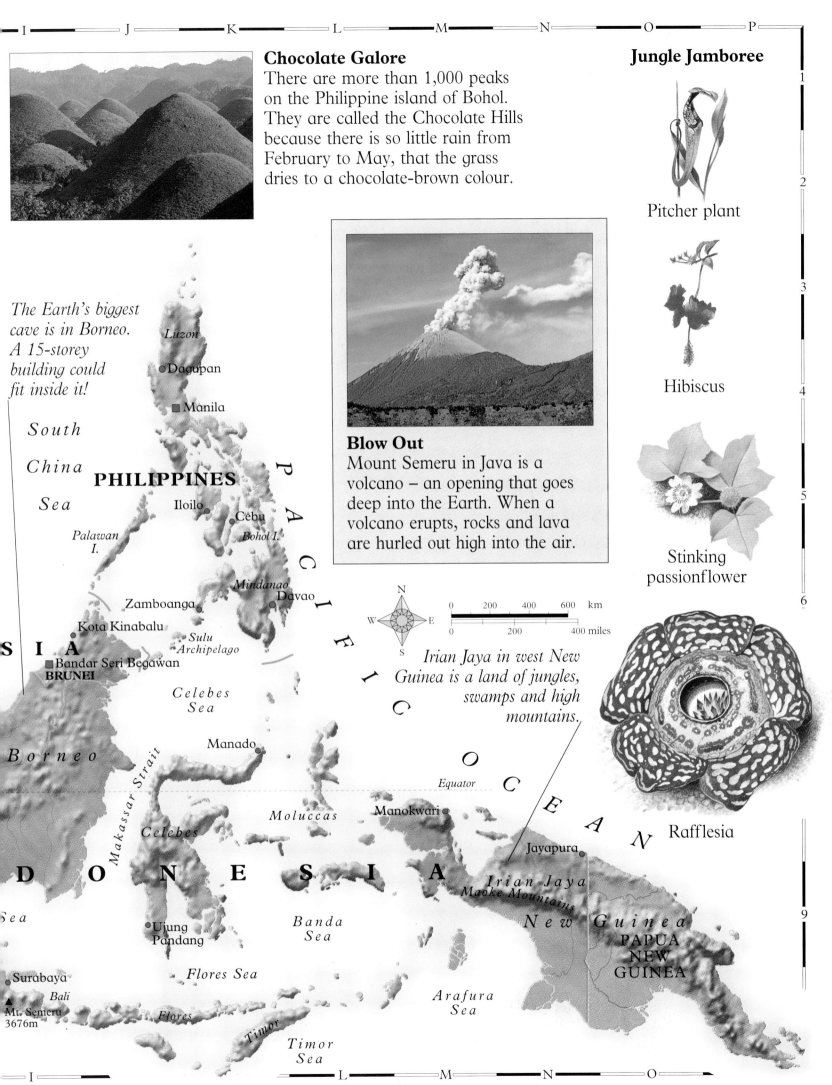

Chocolate Galore

There are more than 1,000 peaks on the Philippine island of Bohol. They are called the Chocolate Hills because there is so little rain from February to May, that the grass dries to a chocolate-brown colour.

Jungle Jamboree

Pitcher plant

Hibiscus

Stinking passionflower

Rafflesia

The Earth's biggest cave is in Borneo. A 15-storey building could fit inside it!

Blow Out

Mount Semeru in Java is a volcano – an opening that goes deep into the Earth. When a volcano erupts, rocks and lava are hurled out high into the air.

Irian Jaya in west New Guinea is a land of jungles, swamps and high mountains.

South China Sea

PHILIPPINES

Luzon

Dagupan

Manila

Iloilo

Cebu

Bohol I.

Palawan I.

Mindanao
Davao

Zamboanga

Kota Kinabalu

Sulu Archipelago

Bandar Seri Begawan
BRUNEI

Celebes Sea

Borneo

Manado

Makassar Strait

Celebes

Moluccas

Manokwari

Equator

Jayapura

Irian Jaya
Maoke Mountains

New Guinea

PAPUA NEW GUINEA

Ujung Pandang

Banda Sea

Surabaya

Bali

Mt. Semeru
3676m

Flores Sea

Flores

Timor

Arafura Sea

Timor Sea

N
W   E
S

| 0 | 200 | 400 | 600 | km |
| 0 | | 200 | | 400 miles |

PACIFIC OCEAN

...SIA

...DONESIA

AUSTRALIA

There are seven large landmasses, or continents, on Earth. Australia is the flattest and smallest of these continents, but it is still big enough for 23 countries the size of Italy to fit inside it! About two-thirds of Australia is covered by deserts and plains, known as the bush or outback. Rain falls on the coasts but rarely reaches the drier inland areas.

Magical Hill
Rising suddenly from the desert floor, Ayers Rock seems to change colour as the sun moves. It is sacred to the Aboriginal people, who call it Uluru.

Shrinking Rock
These boulders in the Tanami Desert are shrinking. They expand in the hot midday sun and contract at night when it cools. Slowly, the outer layers crack and fall off.

Rains and winds batter the north coast. In 1974, a cyclone blasted through Darwin.

Melville I.

INDIAN OCEAN

Timor Sea

Darw

Arn
L

Wyndham

NOR

Broome

Tana
Dese
TER

Great Sandy
Desert

Dampier

Hamersley Range

Tropic of Capricorn

Gibson
Desert

WESTERN

AUST

Uluru
(Ayers Rock)
868m

AUSTRALIA

Great Victoria Desert

Geraldton

A

Kalgoorlie

Perth

Nullarbor Plain

Fremantle

Great
Australian Big

Parts of Australia's 47,070-kilometre coastline have wide, sandy beaches.

Cape
Leeuwin

Albany

Going, Going, Gone
These pillars of rock, or stacks, off the coast of Victoria were formed by waves. Powerful winds called the Roaring Forties caused waves to crash into the cliffs, which crumbled away, leaving these stacks.

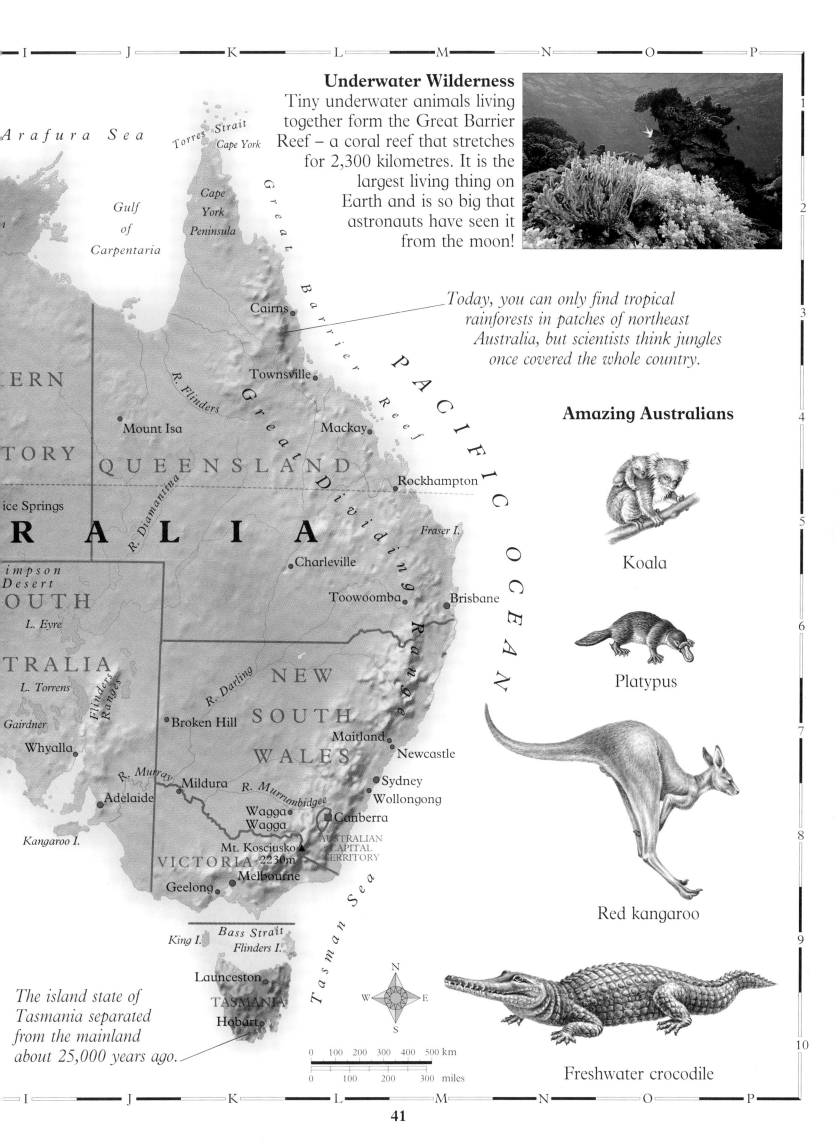

Arafura Sea

Torres Strait

Cape York

Gulf of Carpentaria

Cape York Peninsula

Underwater Wilderness

Tiny underwater animals living together form the Great Barrier Reef – a coral reef that stretches for 2,300 kilometres. It is the largest living thing on Earth and is so big that astronauts have seen it from the moon!

Cairns

Today, you can only find tropical rainforests in patches of northeast Australia, but scientists think jungles once covered the whole country.

Townsville

R. Flinders

ERN

TORY

Mount Isa

Mackay

QUEENSLAND

Great Barrier Reef

Great Dividing Range

Rockhampton

ice Springs

R. Diamantina

RALIA

Fraser I.

impson Desert

Charleville

OUTH

L. Eyre

Toowoomba

Brisbane

TRALIA

L. Torrens

NEW SOUTH WALES

R. Darling

Gairdner

Flinders Ranges

Broken Hill

Whyalla

Maitland

Newcastle

R. Murray

Mildura

R. Murrumbidgee

Sydney

Wollongong

Adelaide

Wagga Wagga

Canberra

Kangaroo I.

Mt. Kosciusko 2230m

AUSTRALIAN CAPITAL TERRITORY

VICTORIA

Melbourne

Geelong

PACIFIC OCEAN

Tasman Sea

Bass Strait

King I.

Flinders I.

Launceston

TASMANIA

The island state of Tasmania separated from the mainland about 25,000 years ago.

Hobart

N
W E
S

Amazing Australians

Koala

Platypus

Red kangaroo

Freshwater crocodile

0 100 200 300 400 500 km

0 100 200 300 miles

New Zealand & the Pacific Islands

Tens of thousands of islands lie between the tropics, in the vast waters of the warm Pacific Ocean. No one lives on most of them and only 3,000 have names. New islands keep popping up as volcanoes erupt from the ocean floor. The weather in this tropical zone is hot and wet. However, places outside this area, such as New Zealand, are said to have a temperate climate because they are cooler.

Northern Mariana Islands (to U.S.A.)

● Saipa

Guam ● Agana
(to U.S.A.)

Koror

MIC

PALAU

Equator

INDONESIA

New Guinea

Bismar Sea

Mt. Wilhelm ▲ PAPU
4506m NEW
GUIN

Port Moresby ▢

Coral Sea

Cor
Sea
Islan
(to Aust

AUSTRALIA

Tropic of Capricorn

Underground Kettle
Beneath Rotorua in New Zealand the ground is so hot that water boils. Steam builds up under the ground and explodes into a huge jet of hot water, called a geyser.

Great Balls of Stone
Each of these enormous balls of ancient rock weighs more than an elephant. No one knows how they reached this beach just north of Dunedin in New Zealand.

Emerald Forests
Rainforests need lots of rain to form. The hilly west coast of New Zealand's South Island is wet enough for thick, temperate rainforests to grow. They are carpeted in damp-loving mosses. The heavy rain is carried in by winds from the stormy Tasman Sea.

Micronesia means small islands and Polynesia means many islands.

Life on the Coral Reef

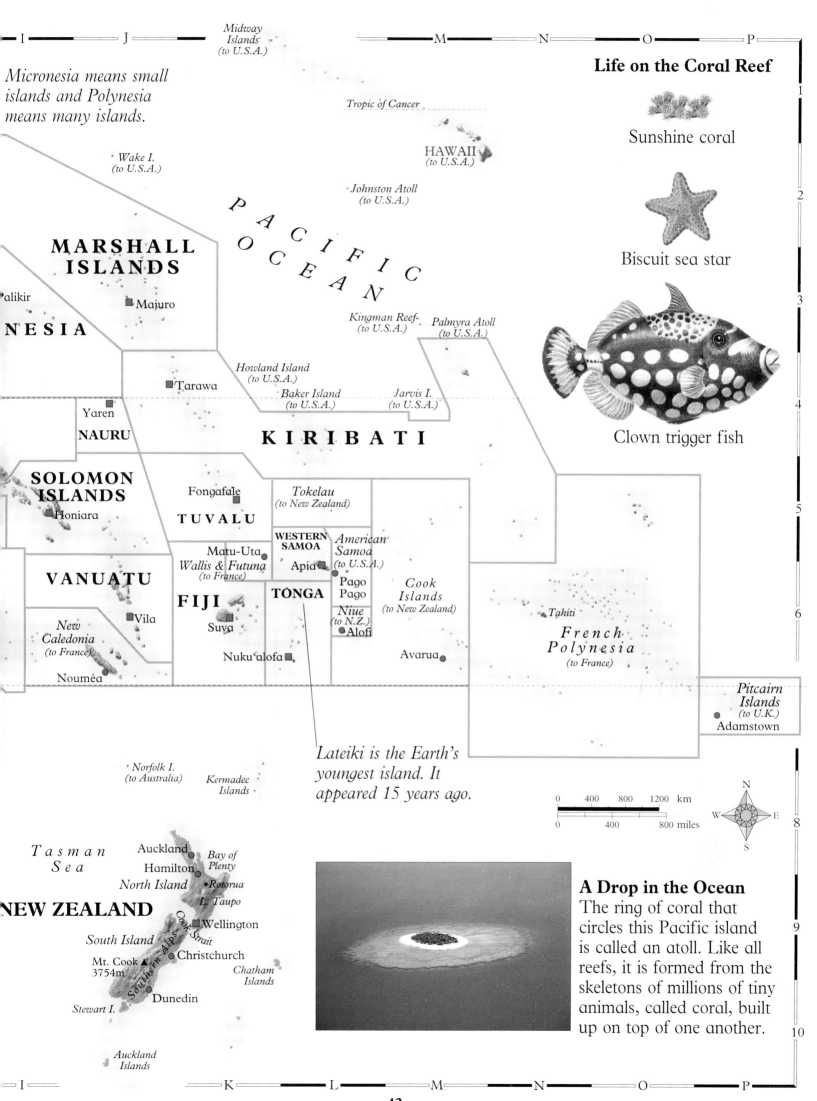

Sunshine coral

Biscuit sea star

Clown trigger fish

P A C I F I C
O C E A N

Tropic of Cancer

Wake I. (to U.S.A.)

HAWAII *(to U.S.A.)*

Johnston Atoll (to U.S.A.)

MARSHALL ISLANDS

alikir ■ Majuro

N E S I A

Kingman Reef (to U.S.A.) *Palmyra Atoll (to U.S.A.)*

Howland Island (to U.S.A.)

■ Tarawa

Baker Island (to U.S.A.) *Jarvis I. (to U.S.A.)*

Yaren ■
NAURU

K I R I B A T I

SOLOMON ISLANDS

■ Honiara

Fongafale ■

TUVALU

Tokelau (to New Zealand)

WESTERN SAMOA *American Samoa (to U.S.A.)*

Matu-Uta ●
Wallis & Futuna (to France)

Apia ■

Pago Pago ●

Cook Islands (to New Zealand)

Tahiti ●

VANUATU

FIJI

TONGA

Niue (to N.Z.)
●Alofi

Avarua ●

French Polynesia (to France)

● Vila

New Caledonia (to France)

Suva ●

Nuku'alofa ■

Nouméa ●

Pitcairn Islands (to U.K.)
● Adamstown

Lateiki is the Earth's youngest island. It appeared 15 years ago.

Norfolk I. (to Australia)

Kermadec Islands

0 400 800 1200 km
0 400 800 miles

N
W   E
S

Tasman Sea

Auckland ●
Hamilton ●
North Island ●Rotorua
Bay of Plenty
L. Taupo

NEW ZEALAND

●Wellington

South Island

Mt. Cook ▲ 3754m
Southern Alps

Christchurch

Cook Strait

Chatham Islands

● Dunedin

Stewart I.

A Drop in the Ocean
The ring of coral that circles this Pacific island is called an atoll. Like all reefs, it is formed from the skeletons of millions of tiny animals, called coral, built up on top of one another.

Auckland Islands

INDEX

A

Aberdeen Scotland, U.K. 25 K2
Abidjan Ivory Coast 18 F9
Abu Dhabi United Arab Emirates 31 N7
Abuja Nigeria 18 G8
Acapulco Mexico 14 G8
Accra Ghana 18 F9
Aconcagua, Mt. Argentina 17 L7
Adamawa Highlands Cameroon 18 G8
Adamstown Pitcairn Islands, Pacific Ocean 43 P7
Adana Turkey 31 I3
Adare, Cape Antarctica 9 L8
Addis Ababa Ethiopia 19 K8
Adelaide Australia 41 J8
Aden Yemen 31 K10
Aden, Gulf of Somalia/Yemen 19 M7 & 31 L10
Afghanistan Country Asia 32 E9
Agadez Niger 18 G7
Agalega Islands Mauritian territory Indian Ocean 21 M5
Agana Guam, Pacific Ocean 42 H2
Agra India 35 K4
Ahaggar Mountains Algeria 18 G6
Ahmadabad India 35 I5
Ahvāz Iran 31 L5
Ajaccio Corsica, France 25 N8
Aktyubinsk Kazakhstan 32 D7
Akureyri Iceland 22 D6
Al' Azīzīyah Libya 18 H4
Al Başrah Iraq 31 L5
Alabama State U.S.A. 13 L7
Alabama R. U.S.A. 13 L7
Åland Islands Finland 23 M7
Alaska State U.S.A. 12 C7
Alaska, Gulf of U.S.A. 10 D6 & 12 D7
Alaska Peninsula U.S.A. 12 C8
Alaska Range Mountains U.S.A. 12 C7
Albania Country Europe 28 F9
Albany Australia 40 E8
Albany R. Canada 11 J7
Alberta Province Canada 10 G7
Ålborg Denmark 23 J9
Ålesund Norway 23 J6
Aleutian Islands U.S.A. 12 A8
Alexandria Egypt 19 J4
Algeria Country Africa 18 F4
Algiers Algeria 18 G3
Alice Springs Australia 41 I5
Allahabad India 35 L5
Alma-Ata Kazakhstan 32 F8
Alofi Niue, Pacific Ocean 43 L6
Alps Mountains Europe 25 M7 & 27 J5
Altai Mountains Asia 32 G7 & 36 F2
Altiplano Region Bolivia 17 K4
Amazon, R. South America 17 L3
Amazonia South America 17 L3
American Samoa U.S.A. territory Pacific Ocean 43 L5
Amirante Islands Seychelles 21 M4
Amman Jordan 31 J4
Amritsar India 35 J3
Amsterdam Netherlands 25 M4
Amundsen Gulf Canada 10 G4
Amundsen-Scott Research station Antarctica 9 L6
Amur R. China/Russian Federation 33 K7 & 37 L1
Anchorage U.S.A. 12 C7
Andaman Islands Indian territory Indian Ocean 38 D4
Andes Mountains South America 17 K3
Andorra Country Europe 25 L8
Andros I. Bahamas 15 L6
Angara, R. Russian Federation 32 G6
Angel Falls Waterfall Venezuela 17 L1
Angola Country Africa 20 G4 & G5
Anguilla U.K. territory 15 O7
Ankara Turkey 31 I2
Antananarivo Madagascar 21 L7
Antarctic Peninsula Antarctica 9 J5
Antigua & Barbuda Country Caribbean Sea 15 P8
Antwerp Belgium 25 M4
Anvers I. Antarctica 9 I5
Apennines Mountains Italy 27 K6
Apia Western Samoa 43 L5
Appalachian Mts. U.S.A. 13 M6

Araguaia, R. Brazil 17 N4
Araks, R. Iran 31 L2
Aral Sea Lake Kazakhstan/Uzbekistan 32 D7
Argentina Country South America 17 K7
Århus Denmark 23 J9
Arizona State U.S.A. 12 G7
Arkansas State U.S.A. 13 K7
Arkansas, R. U.S.A. 13 J6
Arkhangel'sk Russian Federation 29 I4
Armenia Country Asia 31 K2
Arnhem Land Region Australia 40 H2
Aruba Netherlands territory 15 M9
Ashgabat Turkmenistan 32 D8
Asmara Eritrea 19 L7
Asunción Paraguay 17 M6
Aswân Egypt 19 K5
Atacama Desert Chile 17 L6
Athabasca, L. Canada 10 H6
Athens Greece 28 G10
Atlanta U.S.A. 13 M7
Atlas Mts. Algeria/Morocco 18 E4
Auckland New Zealand 43 K8
Auckland Islands New Zealand 43 J10
Augusta U.S.A. 13 O4
Australia Country Indian/Pacific Ocean 40-41
Australian Capital Territory Australia 41 L8
Austria Country Europe 27 L5
Avarua Cook Islands, Pacific Ocean 43 M6
Ayers Rock see Uluru
Azerbaijan Country Asia 31 L2
Azores Portuguese territory Atlantic Ocean 24 D8

B

Bab el Mandeb Strait Djibouti/Yemen 31 K9
Back R. Canada 11 I5
Baffin Bay Canada/Greenland 8 D8 & 11 L3
Baffin I. Canada 8 C7 & 11 L4
Baghdad Iraq 31 K4
Bahamas Country Caribbean Sea 15 M6
Bahrain Country Asia 31 M6
Baikal, L. Russian Federation 33 I6
Baker I. U.S.A. territory Pacific Ocean 43 L4
Bakhtarān Iran 31 L4
Baku Azerbaijan 31 M2
Balearic Islands Spain 25 L9
Bali Island Indonesia 39 I10
Balkhash, L. Kazakhstan 32 F7
Balsas, R. Mexico 14 G8
Bamako Mali 18 E7
Bandar Seri Begawan Brunei 39 I7
Bandung Indonesia 38 H10
Bangalore India 35 J9
Bangka I. Indonesia 38 G8
Bangkok Thailand 38 F4
Bangladesh Country Asia 35 M5
Bangui Central African Republic 19 I9
Banjul Gambia 18 D7
Banks I. Canada 8 D5 & 10 F3
Barbados Country Atlantic Ocean 15 P9
Barcelona Spain 25 L8
Bari Italy 27 M8
Barrow Strait Canada 11 J3
Basle Switzerland 27 J5
Bass Strait Australia 41 K9
Bătdâmbâng Cambodia 38 G5
Bear Islands Russian Federation 33 M4
Beijing see Peking
Beira Mozambique 21 J7
Beirut Lebanon 31 J4
Belcher Islands Canada 11 K6
Belém Brazil 17 N2
Belfast Northern Ireland, U.K. 25 J3
Belgium Country Europe 25 M5
Belgrade Yugoslavia 28 F8
Belize Country North America 15 J8
Belmopan Belize 15 J8
Belo Horizonte Brazil 17 N5
Belorussia Country Europe 28 G6
Beloye, L. Russian Federation 28 H4
Bengal, Bay of Indian Ocean 35 N6 & 38 E3
Benghazi Libya 19 I4
Benin Country Africa 18 F8

Bergen Norway 23 I7
Bering Strait Russian Federation/U.S.A. 8 E4, 12 B7 & 33 P4
Berlin Germany 27 L2
Bermuda U.K. territory Atlantic Ocean 7 N4
Bern Switzerland 27 J5
Bhutan Country Asia 35 M4
Bilbao Spain 25 K8
Bioko Island Equatorial Guinea 20 F2
Birmingham England, U.K. 25 K4
Birmingham U.S.A. 13 L7
Biscay, Bay of France/Spain 25 K7
Bishkek Kyrgyzstan 32 F8
Bismarck U.S.A. 13 J3
Bissau Guinea-Bissau 18 D7
Black Forest Germany 27 J4
Blantyre Malawi 21 J6
Bloemfontein South Africa 21 I9
Blue Nile River Ethiopia/Sudan 19 K9
Bogotá Colombia 17 K2
Bohai, Gulf of China 37 K5
Bohol I. Philippines 39 K5
Boise U.S.A. 12 G4
Bolivia Country South America 17 L5
Bologna Italy 27 K6
Bombay India 35 I7
Bonn Germany 27 I3
Boothia, Gulf of Canada 11 J3
Bordeaux France 25 K7
Borneo Island Indonesia/Malaysia 39 I7
Bornholm Island Denmark 23 L10
Bosnia-Herzegovina Country Europe 28 E8
Boston U.S.A. 13 O5
Bothnia, Gulf of Finland/Sweden 23 M6
Botswana Country Africa 20 H7
Brahmaputra, R. Bangladesh/China/India 35 N4 & 36 F7
Brasília Brazil 17 N4
Bratislava Slovakia 27 M4
Brazil Country South America 17 K3
Brazilian Highlands Brazil 17 N5
Brazzaville Congo 20 G4
Bremen Germany 27 J2
Bridgetown Barbados 15 P9
Brisbane Australia 41 M6
Bristol England, U.K. 25 K4
British Columbia Province Canada 10 F7
Brno Czech Republic 27 M4
Broken Hill Australia 41 J7
Brooks Range Mountains U.S.A. 12 C6
Broome Australia 40 F3
Brunei Country Asia 39 I7
Brussels Belgium 25 M5
Bucharest Romania 28 G7
Budapest Hungary 28 F8
Buenos Aires Argentina 17 M7
Bujumbura Burundi 21 I4
Bulawayo Zimbabwe 21 I7
Bulgaria Country Europe 28 G9
Buraydah Saudi Arabia 31 K6
Burkina Country Africa 18 F8
Burma Country Asia 38 E2
Bursa Turkey 30 H2
Burundi Country Africa 21 I3
Bydgoszcz Poland 27 M2

C

Cabinda Angolan territory Africa 20 G4
Cabora Bassa L. Mozambique 21 J6
Cádiz, Gulf of Spain 25 J10
Cagliari Sardinia, Italy 27 J9
Cairns Australia 41 L3
Cairo Egypt 19 K4
Calcutta India 35 M5
Calgary Canada 10 H7
Cali Colombia 17 K2
California State U.S.A. 12 F6
California, Gulf of Mexico 14 E4
Cambodia Country Asia 38 G4
Cameroon Country Africa 18 G9
Campeche, Bay of Mexico 15 I7
Canada Country North America 10-11
Canadian Shield Canada 11 J6
Canary Islands Spanish territory Atlantic Ocean 24 F9
Canaveral, Cape U.S.A. 13 M8
Canberra Australia 41 L8
Cantábrica Mountains Spain 25 J8
Canton China 37 J8

Cape Cod Peninsula U.S.A. 13 O5
Cape Town South Africa 20 H10
Cape Verde Country Atlantic Ocean 18 B7
Cape York Peninsula Australia 41 K2
Cappadocia Turkey 31 J2
Caquetá, R. Brazil/Colombia 17 K2
Caracas Venezuela 17 L1
Cardiff Wales, U.K. 25 K4
Carpathian Mts. Europe 28 F7
Carpentaria, Gulf of Australia 41 J2
Carson City U.S.A. 12 F5
Casablanca Morocco 18 E4
Cascade Range Mountains U.S.A. 12 F4
Caspian Sea Lake Asia/Europe 29 J8, 31 M2 & 32 D8
Catania Sicily, Italy 27 L10
Caucasus Mountains Asia/Europe 29 I9
Cayenne French Guiana 17 M2
Cayman Islands U.K. territory Caribbean Sea 15 K7
Cebu Philippines 39 K5
Cedros I. Mexico 14 D5
Celebes Island Indonesia 39 J8
Central African Republic Country Africa 19 I8
Central Siberian Plateau Russian Federation 32 G4
Ceuta Spanish territory Africa 18 E3
Chad Country Africa 19 I7
Chad, L. Africa 18 H7
Changchun China 37 M3
Changsha China 37 J7
Channel Islands U.K. 25 K5
Chapala, L. Mexico 14 F7
Charleville Australia 41 L5
Chatham Islands New Zealand 43 K9
Chelyabinsk Russian Federation 32 E6
Chengdu China 37 I6
Chernobyl Ukraine 28 H7
Cherrapunji India 35 N5
Cheyenne U.S.A. 13 I5
Chiang Mai Thailand 38 F3
Chiapa R. Mexico 15 I8
Chicago U.S.A. 13 L5
Chidley, Cape Canada 11 M6
Chihuahua Mexico 14 F5
Chile Country South America 17 K8
Chiloé I. Chile 17 K8
China Country Asia 36 E4
Chiriquí, Gulf of Panama 15 K10
Chişinău Moldavia 28 G8
Chita Russian Federation 33 I6
Chittagong Bangladesh 35 N6
Chitungwiza Zimbabwe 21 J7
Chongqing China 37 I7
Christchurch New Zealand 43 J9
Churchill Canada 11 J6
Cincinnati U.S.A. 13 M5
Citlaltépetl Mountain Mexico 14 H7
Ciudad Juárez Mexico 14 F4
Cleveland U.S.A. 13 M5
Coast Ranges Mountains U.S.A. 12 F4
Coco, R. Honduras 15 K8
Cologne Germany 27 I3
Colombia Country South America 17 K2
Colombo Sri Lanka 35 K10
Colorado State U.S.A. 13 I6
Colorado, R. Argentina 17 L8
Colorado R. Mexico/U.S.A. 12 G7
Columbia U.S.A. 13 M7
Columbia R. Canada/U.S.A. 12 F4
Como, L. Italy 27 J5
Comoros Country Indian Ocean 21 L5
Conakry Guinea 18 D8
Conchos, R. Mexico 14 F5
Congo Country Africa 20
Congo Basin Congo/Zaire 20 H3
Congo, R. Africa 20 G4
Connecticut State U.S.A. 13 O5
Constantine Algeria 18 G3
Cook Islands New Zealand territory Pacific Ocean 43 M6
Cook, Mt. New Zealand 43 J9
Cook Strait New Zealand 43 K9
Copenhagen Denmark 23 K10
Coral Sea Islands Australian territory Pacific Ocean 42 H6
Córdoba Argentina 17 L7
Cork Republic of Ireland 25 I4
Coronado Bay Costa Rica 15 J10
Corsica French territory Mediterranean Sea 25 M8

Costa Rica *Country* North America 15 J9
Cozumel I. Mexico 15 J7
Crete *Island* Greece 28 G10
Croatia *Country* Europe 28 E8
Cuanza, R. Angola 20 G5
Cuba *Country* Caribbean Sea 15 L6
Cunene R. Angola/Namibia 20 G6
Curitiba Brazil 17 N6
Cyprus *Country* Mediterranean Sea 31 I4
Czech Republic *Country* Europe 27 L4

D

Da Nang Vietnam 38 H4
Dacca Bangladesh 35 N5
Dagupan Philippines 39 J4
Dakar Senegal 18 D7
Dallas U.S.A. 13 J7
Dampier Australia 40 E4
Danakil Depression Ethiopia 19 L7
Danube, R. Europe 27 K4 & 28 G7
Dar es Salaam Tanzania 21 K4
Darien, Gulf of Colombia/Panama 15 L10 & 17 K1
Darling, R. Australia 41 K7
Darwin Australia 40 H2
Davao Philippines 39 K6
Davis Strait Canada/Greenland 8 C8 & 11 M4
Dawson Canada 10 E5
Dead Sea *Lake* Israel/Jordan 31 J5
Death Valley U.S.A. 12 G6
Deccan Plateau India 35 J7
Delaware *State* U.S.A. 13 N6
Delgado, Cape Mozambique 21 K5
Denali (Mt. McKinley) *Mountain* U.S.A. 12 C7
Denmark *Country* Europe 23 J9
Denmark Strait Greenland/Iceland 9 E9
Denver U.S.A. 13 I5
Des Moines U.S.A. 13 K5
Detroit U.S.A. 13 M5
Devon I. Canada 11 K3
Diamantina, R. Australia 41 J5
Djibouti *Country* Africa 19 L7
Djibouti Djibouti 19 L8
Dnieper, R. Europe 28 H7
Dodoma Tanzania 21 J4
Doha Qatar 31 M6
Dominica *Country* Caribbean Sea 15 P8
Dominican Republic *Country* Caribbean Sea 15 O7
Don, R. Russian Federation 29 I7
Dordogne, R. France 25 L7
Dortmund Germany 27 J3
Douro, R. Portugal 25 I8
Drakensberg Mts. Lesotho/South Africa 21 I10
Drau, R. Europe 27 L5
Dresden Germany 27 L3
Dubai United Arab Emirates 31 N6
Dubawnt, L. Canada 11 I5
Dublin Republic of Ireland 25 J4
Dunedin New Zealand 43 J10
Durban South Africa 21 J9
Dushanbe Tajikistan 32 E8
Düsseldorf Germany 27 I3
Dvina R., Northern Russian Federation 29 I1
Dvina R., Western Europe 28 G6

E

Easter I. *Chilean territory* Pacific Ocean 7 L8
Eastern Ghats *Mountains* India 35 K8
Eastmain R. Canada 11 L7
Ebro, R. Spain 25 K8
Ecuador *Country* South America 17 J3
Edinburgh Scotland, U.K. 25 K3
Edmonton Canada 10 H7
Egypt *Country* Africa 19 J5
El Aaiún Western Sahara 18 D5
El Salvador *Country* North America 15 I9
Elba *Island* Italy 27 J7
Elbe, R. Germany 27 K2
El'brus, Mt. Russian Federation 29 I9
Elburz Mts. Iran 31 M3
Ellesmere I. Canada 8 D7 & 11 L2
Ellsworth Mts. Antarctica 9 K6

Ems, R. Germany 27 J2
Enderby Land *Region* Antarctica 9 M5
England *Region* U.K. 25 K4
English Channel France/U.K. 25 K5
Equatorial Guinea *Country* Africa 20 F3
Erebus, Mt. Antarctica 9 L7
Erie, L. Canada/U.S.A. 11 K9 & 13 M5
Eritrea *Country* Africa 19 L7
Esbjerg Denmark 23 J10
Eşfahān Iran 31 M4
Essen Germany 27 I3
Estonia *Country* Europe 28 G5
Ethiopia *Country* Africa 19 K8
Ethiopian Highlands Ethiopia 19 K8
Etna *Mountain* Sicily, Italy 27 L9
Euphrates, R. Asia 31 K4
Everest, Mt. China/Nepal 35 M4 & 36 F7
Everglades *Wetland* U.S.A. 13 M9
Eyre, L. Australia 41 I6

F

Faeroe Islands *Danish territory* Atlantic Ocean 22 E6
Faial *Island* Azores, Atlantic Ocean 24 D9
Fairbanks U.S.A. 12 D7
Faisalabad Pakistan 35 I3
Falcon L. Mexico/U.S.A. 14 G5
Falkland Islands *U.K. territory* Atlantic Ocean 17 M10
Farvel, Cape Greenland 9 C9
Fdérik Mauritania 18 D6
Fianarantsoa Madagascar 21 L7
Fiji *Country* Pacific Ocean 43 K6
Finland *Country* Europe 23 N3
Finland, Gulf of Europe 23 N7 & 28 G5
Fish, R. Namibia 20 G8
Flinders I. Australia 41 K9
Flinders Ranges *Mountains* Australia 41 J7
Flinders, R. Australia 41 J4
Florence Italy 27 K7
Flores *Island* Azores, Atlantic Ocean 24 D8
Flores *Island* Indonesia 39 J10
Florida *State* U.S.A. 13 M8
Florida, Straits of Cuba/U.S.A. 15 K6
Fongafale Tuvalu, Pacific Ocean 43 K5
Fort Peck, L. U.S.A. 12 H3
Fortaleza Brazil 17 O3
France *Country* Europe 25 K6
Frankfurt am Main Germany 27 J3
Franz Josef Land *Island group* Russian Federation 8 G7
Fraser R. Canada 10 G7
Fraser I. Australia 41 M5
Freetown Sierra Leone 18 D8
Fremantle Australia 40 E7
French Guiana *French territory* South America 17 M2
French Polynesia *French territory* Pacific Ocean 43 N6
Fria, Cape Namibia 20 F6
Fuerteventura *Island* Canary Islands, Atlantic Ocean 24 G9
Fuji, Mt. Japan 37 N5
Fukuoka Japan 37 M6
Fundy, Bay of Canada 11 M9
Fuzhou China 31 K7

G

Gabon *Country* Africa 20 F3
Gaborone Botswana 21 I8
Gairdner, L. Australia 41 I7
Galapagos Islands *Ecuadorian terrritory* Pacific Ocean 17 I3
Gambia *Country* Africa 18 C7
Ganges Delta Bangladesh 35 N6
Ganges, R. Bangladesh/India 35 K4
Garda, L. Italy 27 K6
Garonne, R. France 25 K7
Garry, L. Canada 11 J5
Gävle Sweden 23 M7
Gaziantep Turkey 31 J3
Gdańsk Poland 27 M1
Geelong Australia 41 K9
Geneva Switzerland 27 I5
Geneva, L. France/Switzerland 25 M6 & 27 I5
Genoa Italy 27 J6
Genoa, Gulf of Italy 27 J7

Georgetown Guyana 17 M1
Georgia *Country* Asia 29 I9
Georgia *State* U.S.A. 13 M7
Geraldton Australia 40 D6
Germany *Country* Europe 27 J3
Ghana *Country* Africa 18 F8
Giant's Causeway Northern Ireland, U.K. 25 I3
Gibraltar *U.K. territory* Mediterranean Sea 25 J10
Gibraltar, Strait of Morocco/Spain 25 J10
Gibson Desert Australia 40 G5
Giza Egypt 19 K4
Glåma, R. Norway 23 K6
Glasgow Scotland, U.K. 25 J3
Gobi Desert China/Mongolia 32 H8 & 36 H4
Godavari, R. India 35 K7
Godthåb Greenland 9 C9
Golan Heights *Disputed territory* Syria 31 J4
Good Hope, Cape of South Africa 20 H10
Göteborg Sweden 23 K8
Gotland *Island* Sweden 23 M8
Grampian Mts. Scotland, U.K. 25 J2
Gran Canaria *Island* Canary Islands, Atlantic Ocean 24 G9
Grand Bahama I. Bahamas 15 K5
Grand Canyon U.S.A. 12 G6
Grande, R. Mexico/U.S.A. 13 I7 & 14 G4
Graz Austria 27 L5
Great Abaco I. Bahamas 15 L5
Great Australian Bight *Bay* Australia 40 H7
Great Bahama Bank *Sea feature* Caribbean Sea 15 L6
Great Bahama I. Bahamas 15 K5
Great Barrier Reef Australia 41 K2
Great Basin U.S.A. 12 F5
Great Bear L. Canada 10 G5
Great Dividing Range *Mountains* Australia 41 K4
Great Lakes Canada/U.S.A. 11 K8 & 13 L4
Great Plain of China China 37 K6
Great Plains U.S.A. 13 I4
Great Rift Valley Africa/Asia 20 I3
Great Salt Desert Iran 31 M4
Great Salt L. U.S.A. 12 G5
Great Sandy Desert Australia 40 F4
Great Slave L. Canada 10 H5
Great Victoria Desert Australia 40 F6
Greater Antilles *Island group* Caribbean Sea 15 K7
Greater Khingan Range *Mountains* China 37 K3
Greece *Country* Europe 28 F9
Greenland *Danish territory* Atlantic Ocean 8 D8
Grenada *Country* Caribbean Sea 15 P9
Grotte de Clamouse *Cave* France 25 I7
Guadalajara Mexico 14 G7
Guadalquivir, R. Spain 25 J10
Guadalupe I. Mexico 14 D4
Guadeloupe *French territory* Caribbean Sea 15 P8
Guadiana, R. Portugal/Spain 25 J9
Guam *U.S.A. territory* Pacific Ocean 42 G2
Guatemala *Country* North America 15 I8
Guatemala City Guatemala 15 I8
Guayaquil Ecuador 17 J3
Guiana Highlands South America 17 L2
Guilin Hills China 37 J7
Guinea *Country* Africa 18 D8
Guinea, Gulf of Africa 18 F9
Guinea-Bissau *Country* Africa 18 C8
Guiyang China 37 I7
Guyana *Country* South America 17 M1

H

Hague, The Netherlands 25 M4
Hai Phong Vietnam 38 H3
Hainan *Island* China 37 J9
Haiti *Country* Caribbean Sea 15 M7
Ḩalab Syria 31 J3
Halifax Canada 11 M9
Hamburg Germany 27 K2

Hamersley Range *Mountains* Australia 40 D4
Hamilton New Zealand 43 K8
Hamilton Canada 11 L9
Hanoi Vietnam 38 G3
Hanover Germany 27 J2
Harare Zimbabwe 21 J6
Harbin China 37 M3
Hardanger Fjord Norway 23 I7
Hargeysa Somalia 19 L8
Havana Cuba 15 K6
Hawaii *Island* Hawaii, Pacific Ocean 12 D10
Hawaii *State* U.S.A. 12 C10
Helena U.S.A. 12 H3
Helsinki Finland 23 O7
Herāt Afghanistan 32 E9
Himalayas *Mountains* China/India/Nepal 35 J2 & 36 E6
Hindu Kush *Mountains* Afghanistan 32 E9
Hiroshima Japan 37 N6
Ho Chi Minh City Vietnam 38 H5
Hobart Australia 41 K10
Hokkaidō *Island* Japan 37 O3
Holguín Cuba 15 L7
Honduras *Country* North America 15 J8
Honduras, Gulf of North America 15 J8
Hong Kong *U.K. territory* Asia 37 K8
Hongshui R. China 37 I8
Honiara Solomon Islands 43 I5
Honolulu Oahu I. Hawaii, Pacific Ocean 12 D9
Honshū *Island* Japan 37 O5
Hormuz, Strait of Iran/Oman 31 N6
Horn, Cape Chile 17 L10
Houston U.S.A. 13 K8
Howland I. *U.S.A. territory* Pacific Ocean 43 K4
Huambo Angola 20 G6
Hudson R. U.S.A. 13 N5
Hudson Bay Canada 11 K6
Hudson Strait Canada 11 L5
Hulun L. China 37 K2
Hungary *Country* Europe 28 F8
Huron, L. Canada/U.S.A. 11 K8 & 13 M4
Hyderabad India 35 K7
Hyderabad Pakistan 34 H5

I

Iberian Peninsula Europe 25 J9
Iceland *Country* Atlantic Ocean 22 D6
Idaho *State* U.S.A. 12 G4
Illinois *State* U.S.A. 13 L5
Iloilo Philippines 39 J5
Inari, L. Finland 23 N2
India *Country* Asia 35 I5
Indiana *State* U.S.A. 13 L5
Indonesia *Country* Asia 38 G9
Indus, R. Asia 34 H5 & 35 I3
Inn, R. Europe 27 K4
Inner Hebrides *Islands* Scotland, U.K. 25 J2
Innsbruck Austria 27 K5
Iowa *State* U.S.A. 13 K5
Iran *Country* Asia 31 M4
Iran, Plateau of Iran 31 M4
Iraq *Country* Asia 31 K5
Ireland, Republic of *Country* Europe 25 I3
Irian Jaya *Region* Indonesia 39 M9
Irkutsk Russian Federation 32 H6
Irrawaddy R. Burma 38 E3
Irtysh, R. Asia 32 E5
Islamabad Pakistan 35 I2
Israel *Country* Asia 31 I4
Issyk-kul', L. Kyrgyzstan 32 F8
Istanbul Turkey 30 H2
Italy *Country* Europe 27 K6
Ivory Coast *Country* Africa 18 E8
Izmir Turkey 30 H3

J

Jabalpur India 35 K5
Jackson U.S.A. 13 L7
Jaffna Sri Lanka 35 K10
Jaipur India 35 J4
Jakarta Indonesia 38 H9

45

Jamaica *Country* Caribbean Sea 15 L7
James Bay Canada 11 K7
Japan *Country* Asia 37 O6
Jarvis I. *U.S.A. territory* Pacific Ocean 43 M4
Java *Island* Indonesia 38 H10
Jayapura Indonesia 39 N8
Jedda Saudi Arabia 31 J7
Jerusalem Israel 31 I5
Johannesburg South Africa 21 I8
Johnston Atoll *U.S.A. territory* Pacific Ocean 43 L2
Jönköping Sweden 23 L8
Jordan *Country* Asia 31 J5
Juba, R. Somalia 19 L9
Jutland *Peninsula* Denmark 23 J9

K

Kabul Afghanistan 32 E9
Kakana Nicobar Islands 38 E6
Kalahari Desert Botswana 20 H8
Kalgoorlie Australia 40 F7
Kaliningrad Russian Federation 28 F6
Kama, R. Russian Federation 29 K6
Kamchatka Peninsula Russian Federation 33 M6
Kampala Uganda 21 J3
Kananga Zaire 20 H4
Kandy Sri Lanka 35 K10
Kangaroo I. Australia 41 I8
Kanpur India 35 K4
Kansas *State* U.S.A. 13 J6
Kansas City U.S.A. 13 K5
Karachi Pakistan 34 H5
Karaganda Kazakhstan 32 F7
Kariba, L. Zambia/Zimbabwe 21 I6
Kasai, R. Angoal/Zaire 20 H5
Kathmandu Nepal 35 M4
Katowice Poland 27 M3
Kauai *Island* Hawaii State, Pacific Ocean 12 C9
Kazakhstan *Country* Asia 32 D7
Kemi Finland 23 N4
Kemi, R. Finland 23 N4
Kentucky *State* U.S.A. 13 L6
Kenya *Country* Africa 21 J3
Kermadec Islands New Zealand 43 K8
Khabarovsk Russian Federation 33 K7
Khartoum Sudan 19 K7
Khyber Pass Afghanistan/Pakistan 32 E9 & 35 I2
Kiev Ukraine 28 H7
Kigali Rwanda 21 I3
Kilimanjaro, Mt. Tanzania 21 K3
King I. Australia 41 K9
Kingman Reef *U.S.A. territory* Pacific Ocean 43 L3
Kingston Jamaica 15 L8
Kirghiz Steppe *Region* Kazakhstan 32 E7
Kinhasa Zaire 20 G4
Kiribati *Country* Pacific Ocean 43 K4
Kirinyaga, Mt. Kenya 21 K3
Kirkuk Iraq 31 K3
Kiruna Sweden 23 M3
Kitwe Zambia 21 I5
Kizilirmak, R. Turkey 31 I2
Kjølen Mountains Norway/Sweden 23 L4
Ko Phi Phi *Island* Malaysia 38 E6
Kōbe Japan 37 N5
Kodiak I. U.S.A. 12 C8
Kola Peninsula Russian Federation 29 I3
Kolguyev I. Russian Federation 29 J2
Kolyma Range *Mountains* Russian Federation 33 M5
Konya Turkey 31 H3
Korean Peninsula North Korea/South Korea 37 M5
Korea Strait Japan/Korea 37 L6
Koror Palau, Pacific Ocean 42 G3
Kosciusko, Mt. Australia 41 L8
Košice Slovakia 27 N4
Kota Kinabalu Malaysia 39 I6
Kowloon Hong Kong 37 K8
Kra, Isthmus of Thailand 38 F5
Krakatau I. Indonesia 38 G9
Kraków Poland 27 N3
Krasnoyarsk Russian Federation 32 G6
Krishna, R. India 35 I7
Kristiansand Norway 23 J8
Kuala Lumpur Malaysia 38 G7
Kuching Malaysia 38 H7
Kunlun Mountains China 36 E5

Kunming China 37 I8
Kuopio Finland 23 O5
Kura, R. Azerbaijan/Georgia 31 L2
Kurile Islands Asia 33 L7 & 37 P3
Kustanai Kazakhstan 32 E6
Kutch, Gulf of India 34 H5
Kuwait *Country* Asia 31 L5
Kuwait City Kuwait 31 L5
Kuybyshev Reservoir Russian Federation 29 J6
Kyōto Japan 37 N5
Kyrgyzstan *Country* Asia 32 E8
Kyūshū *Island* Japan 37 M6

L

La Paz Bolivia 17 L5
Labrador Canada 11 M7
Laccadive Islands *Indian territory* Indian Ocean 34 H8
Ladoga, L. Russian Federation 28 H5
Lågen, R. Norway 23 J6
Lagos Nigeria 18 G8
Lagos Portugal 25 I10
Lahore Pakistan 35 J3
Lambert Glacier Antarctica 9 N5
Lanzarote *Island* Canary Islands, Atlantic Ocean 24 G9
Lanzhou China 37 I5
Laos *Country* Asia 38 F3
Lappland *Region* Finland 23 M3
Las Palmas Gran Canaria Canary Islands, Atlantic Ocean 24 G9
Latvia *Country* Europe 28 G5
Launceston Australia 41 K9
Laurentian Plateau Canada 11 L7
Lebanon *Country* Asia 31 J4
Leeds England, U.K. 25 K3
Leeuwin, Cape Australia 40 E8
Leipzig Germany 27 K3
Lena, R. Russian Federation 33 J4
León Mexico 14 G7
León Nicaragua 15 J9
Lesotho *Country* Africa 21 I9
Lesser Antilles *Island group* Caribbean Sea 15 N9
Lhasa China 36 G7
Liberia *Country* Africa 18 E8
Libreville Gabon 20 F3
Libya *Country* Africa 18 H5
Libyan Desert Africa 19 I5
Liechtenstein *Country* Europe 27 J5
Lille France 25 L5
Lillehammer Norway 23 K7
Lilongwe Malawi 21 J6
Lima Peru 17 K4
Limpopo, R. Africa 21 J7
Linz Austria 27 L4
Lisbon Portugal 25 I9
Lithuania *Country* Europe 28 F6
Little Rock U.S.A. 13 K6
Liverpool England, U.K. 25 K4
Ljubljana Slovenia 28 E8
Łódź Poland 27 N3
Lofoten Islands Norway 23 L3
Loire, R. France 25 L6
Lomé Togo 18 F9
London England, U.K. 25 L4
Long I. U.S.A. 13 O5
Longyearbyen Svalbard, Arctic Ocean 8 F8
Lop Nur L. China 36 F4
Los Angeles U.S.A. 12 F7
Louang Phrabang Laos 38 G3
Louisiana *State* U.S.A. 13 K7
Louisville U.S.A. 13 L6
Lower California *Peninsula* Mexico 14 D4
Lualaba, R. Zaire 21 I3
Luanda Angola 20 G5
Lublin Poland 27 O3
Lubumbashi Zaire 21 I5
Lucknow India 35 K4
Lule, R. Sweden 23 M4
Luleå Sweden 23 N4
Lusaka Zambia 21 I6
Luxembourg *Country* Europe 25 M5
Luzon *Island* Philippines 39 J3
Lyon France 25 M7

M

Macao *Portuguese territory* Asia 37 J8
Macedonia *Country* Europe 28 F9
Mackay Australia 41 L4

Mackenzie Mts. Canada 10 E5
Mackenzie, R. Canada 10 F5
Madagascar *Country* Indian Ocean 21 L8
Madeira *Island* Madeira Islands, Atlantic Ocean 24 F8
Madeira Islands *Portuguese territory* Atlantic Ocean 24 F8
Madeira, R. Bolivia/Brazil 17 L4
Madras India 35 K8
Madrid Spain 25 K9
Magadan Russian Federation 33 L5
Magdalena, R. Colombia 17 K2
Magellan, Strait of Chile 17 L10
Mahé I. Seychelles 21 M4
Main, R. Germany 27 K3
Maine *State* U.S.A. 13 O4
Maitland Australia 41 M7
Majorca *Island* Spain 25 L9
Majuro Marshall Islands, Pacific Ocean 43 J3
Makassar Strait Indonesia 39 J8
Malabo Equatorial Guinea 20 F2
Malacca, Strait of Indonesia/Malaysia 38 F7
Málaga Spain 25 J10
Malawi *Country* Africa 21 J5
Malay Peninsula Asia 38 F6
Malaysia *Country* Asia 38 G6
Maldives *Country* Indian Ocean 34 H9
Male Maldives 34 H9
Mali *Country* Africa 18 F6
Malmö Sweden 23 K10
Malta *Country* Europe 27 L10
Mamoré, R. Bolivia 17 L4
Manado Indonesia 39 K7
Managua Nicaragua 15 J9
Manama Bahrain 31 M6
Manaus Brazil 17 M3
Manchester England, U.K. 25 K4
Manchurian Plain China 37 L3
Mandalay Burma 38 E2
Manila Philippines 39 J4
Manitoba *Province* Canada 11 I7
Manitoba, L. Canada 11 I8
Mannar, Gulf of India/Sri Lanka 35 K10
Manokwari Indonesia 39 M8
Maoke Mountains New Guinea 39 M9
Maputo Mozambique 21 J8
Maracaibo Venezuela 17 K1
Maracaibo, L. Venezuela 17 K1
Marañón, R. Peru 17 K3
Margarita I. Venezuela 17 L1
Mariana Trench Pacific Ocean 4 H6
Marías Islands Mexico 14 E7
Marie Byrd Land *Region* Antarctica 9 K6
Marne, R. France 25 L5
Marrakesh Morocco 18 E4
Marseille France 25 M8
Marshall Islands *Country* Pacific Ocean 43 I2
Martinique *French territory* Caribbean Sea 15 P8
Maryland *State* U.S.A. 13 N6
Maseru Lesotho 21 I9
Mashhad Iran 31 N3
Massachusetts *State* U.S.A. 13 O5
Massif Central France 25 L7
Mato Grosso, Plateau of Brazil 17 M4
Matu-Uta *Wallis & Futuna, Pacific* Ocean 43 K5
Maui *Island* Hawaii State, Pacific Ocean 12 D9
Mauna Loa *Mountain* Maui Hawaii, Pacific Ocean 12 D10
Mauritania *Country* Africa 18 D6
Mauritius *Country* Indian Ocean 21 N7
Mayotte I. *French territory* Indian Ocean 21 L6
Mbabane Swaziland 21 J8
Mbuji-Mayi Zaire 20 H4
McKinley, Mt. *see* Denali
Mecca Saudi Arabia 31 J7
Medan Indonesia 38 F7
Medellín Colombia 17 K1
Medina Saudi Arabia 31 I7
Mekong R. Asia 36 H6 & 38 G3
Mekong Delta Vietnam 38 G5
Melbourne Australia 41 K8
Melilla *Spanish territory* Africa 18 F3
Melville I. Australia 40 H1
Melville I. Canada 10 H3
Mérida Mexico 15 J7
Mesopotamia *Region* Iraq/Syria 31 K3

Meuse, R. Europe 25 M5
Mexican Plateau Mexico 14 F5
Mexico *Country* South America 14 F6
Mexico City Mexico 14 H7
Mexico, Gulf of Mexico/U.S.A. 13 K8 & 15 I6
Miami U.S.A. 13 M9
Michigan *State* U.S.A. 13 L4
Michigan, L. U.S.A. 11 K9 & 13 L5
Micronesia *Country* Pacific Ocean 42 H3
Midway Islands *U.S.A. territory* Pacific Ocean 43 K1
Milan Italy 27 J6
Mildura Australia 41 J8
Milwaukee U.S.A. 13 L4
Mindanao *Island* Philippines 39 K6
Minneapolis U.S.A. 13 K4
Minnesota *State* U.S.A. 13 K3
Minsk Belorussia 28 G6
Mississippi R. U.S.A. 13 L7
Mississippi *State* U.S.A. 13 L7
Mississippi Delta U.S.A. 13 L8
Missouri R. U.S.A. 13 K5
Missouri *State* U.S.A. 13 K6
Mjøsa, L. Norway 23 K7
Mogadishu Somalia 19 M9
Moldavia *Country* Europe 28 G8
Moluccas *Islands* Indonesia 39 K8
Mombasa Kenya 21 K4
Monaco *Country* Europe 25 N7
Mongolia *Country* Asia 32 H7
Monrovia Liberia 18 E8
Mont Blanc *Mountain* France 25 M7
Mont St. Michel *Island* France 25 K5
Montana *State* U.S.A. 12 H4
Monterrey Mexico 14 G5
Montevideo Uruguay 17 M7
Montreal Canada 11 L8
Montserrat *U.K. territory* Caribbean Sea 15 P8
Monument Valley U.S.A. 12 H6
Morocco *Country* Africa 18 E4
Moroni Comoros 21 L5
Moscow Russian Federation 29 I6
Mosul Iraq 31 K3
Moulmein Burma 38 F4
Mount Isa Australia 41 J4
Mozambique *Country* Africa 21 J7
Mozambique Channel Madagascar/Mozambique 21 K7
Multan Pakistan 35 I3
Munich Germany 27 K4
Muonio, R. Sweden 23 N3
Murray, R. Australia 41 J7
Murrumbidgee, R. Australia 41 K8
Muscat Oman 31 N7
Mweru, L. Zaire/Zambia 21 I5

N

Nafud Desert Saudi Arabia 31 K5
Nagasaki Japan 37 M6
Nagoya Japan 37 N5
Nagpur India 35 K6
Nairobi Kenya 21 J3
Nakhon Si Thammarat Thailand 38 F6
Namib Desert Namibia 20 G7
Namibia *Country* Africa 20 G7
Nanchang China 37 K7
Nanjing China 37 K6
Nantes France 25 K6
Naples Italy 27 L8
Nares Strait Canada 11 L2
Narmada, R. India 35 J6
Narvik Norway 23 M3
Nashville U.S.A. 13 L6
Nassau Bahamas 15 L6
Nasser, L. Egypt/Sudan 19 J6
Nauru *Country* Pacific Ocean 43 J4
N'Djamena Chad 18 H7
Ndola Zambia 21 I5
Nebraska *State* U.S.A. 13 I5
Negro R. Brazil 17 L2
Nelson R. Canada 11 J7
Nepal *Country* Asia 35 K4
Netherlands *Country* Europe 25 N4
Netherlands Antilles *Netherlands territory* 15 N9
Neusiedler L. Austria/Hungary 27 L4
Nevada *State* U.S.A. 12 F6
New Brunswick *Province* Canada 11 M8
New Caledonia *French territory* Pacific Ocean 43 I6

New Delhi India 35 J4
New Guinea *Island* Indonesia/Papua New Guinea 39 N9, 42 G4
New Hampshire *State* U.S.A. 13 O4
New Jersey *State* U.S.A. 13 N5
New Mexico *State* U.S.A. 13 I7
New Orleans U.S.A. 13 L8
New Siberian Islands Russian Federation 8 G5 & 33 L3
New South Wales *State* Australia 41 K6
New York *State* U.S.A. 13 N4
New York U.S.A. 13 O5
New Zealand *Country* Pacific Ocean 43 I9
Newcastle Australia 41 M7
Newcastle upon Tyne England, U.K. 25 K3
Newfoundland *Island* Canada 11 N8
Newfoundland *Province* Canada 11 M6
Niagara Falls *Waterfall* Canada/U.S.A. 11 L9 & 13 N5
Niamey Niger 18 F7
Nicaragua *Country* North America 15 J9
Nicaragua, L. Nicaragua 15 K9
Nice France 25 M7
Nicobar Islands *Indian territory* Indian Ocean 38 E6
Nicosia Cyprus 31 I4
Niger *Country* Africa 18 G6
Niger, R. Africa 18 G8
Nigeria *Country* Africa 18 G8
Niigata Japan 37 O5
Nile Delta Egypt 19 J4
Nile, R. Africa 19 K6
Nipigon, L. Canada 11 K8
Niue *New Zealand territory* Pacific Ocean 43 L6
Nizhniy Novgorod Russian Federation 29 J6
Norfolk I. *Australian territory* Pacific Ocean 43 J7
Norrköping Sweden 23 L8
North Cape Norway 23 N1
North Carolina *State* U.S.A. 13 N6
North Dakota *State* U.S.A. 13 I3
North European Plain Europe 27 K2 & 28 H6
North Island New Zealand 43 J9
North Korea *Country* Asia 37 L4
North Pole Arctic Ocean 8 F7
Northern Ireland *Region* U.K. 25 J3
Northern Mariana Islands *U.S.A. territory* Pacific Ocean 42 H2
Northern Territory Australia 40 H4
Northwest Territories *Province* Canada 10 G4
Norway *Country* Europe 23 J7
Nouakchott Mauritania 18 D6
Nouméa New Caledonia, Pacific Ocean 43 J7
Nova Scotia *Province* Canada 11 M9
Novaya Zemlya *Island group* Russian Federation 29 K1
Novosibirsk Russian Federation 32 F6
Nubian Desert Sudan 19 K6
Nuku'alofa Tonga, Pacific Ocean 43 L6
Nullarbor Plain Australia 40 G7
Nuremberg Germany 27 K4
Nyasa, L. Africa 21 J5

O

Oahe, L. U.S.A. 13 J4
Oahu *Island* Hawaii State, Pacific Ocean 12 D9
Ob', R. Russian Federation 32 E4
Odense Denmark 23 J10
Oder, R. Germany 27 L2
Odesa Ukraine 28 H8
Odra, R. Poland 27 M3
Ohio *State* U.S.A. 13 M5
Ohio R. U.S.A. 13 L6
Okavango Delta Botswana 20 H7
Okavango, R. Africa 20 G6
Okeechobee, L. U.S.A. 13 M8
Okinawa *Island* Japan 37 L7
Oklahoma *State* U.S.A. 13 J7
Oklahoma City U.S.A. 13 J6
Öland *Island* Sweden 23 M9
Omaha U.S.A. 13 K5
Oman *Country* Asia 31 N8
Oman, Gulf of Iran/Oman 31 N7
Omdurman Sudan 19 K7

Omsk Russian Federation 32 F6
Onega, L. Russian Federation 28 H4
Ontario *Province* Canada 11 J7
Ontario, L. Canada/U.S.A. 11 L9 & 13 N4
Oran Algeria 18 F3
Orange R. Africa 20 H9
Oregon *State* U.S.A. 12 F5
Orinoco, R. Venezuela 17 L2
Orkney Islands U.K. 25 K1
Orléans France 25 L6
Ōsaka Japan 37 N5
Osh Kyrgyzstan 32 F8
Oslo Norway 23 K7
Östersund Sweden 23 L6
Ostrava Czech Republic 27 M4
Ottawa Canada 11 L8
Ottawa R. Canada 11 L8
Ouagadougou Burkina 18 F7
Oulu Finland 23 N4
Oulu, L. Finland 23 O5
Outer Hebrides *Island group* U.K. 25 I2

P

Padang Indonesia 38 F8
Pago Pago American Samoa, Pacific Ocean 43 L6
Paine Horns Chile 17 K10
Pakistan *Country* Asia 34 G4
Palau *Country* Pacific Ocean 42 G3
Palawan I. Philippines 39 J5
Palembang Indonesia 38 G9
Palermo Sicily, Italy 27 L9
Palikir Micronesia 43 I3
Palmyra Atoll *U.S.A. territory* Pacific Ocean 43 M3
Pampas *Region* Argentina 17 L7
Pamukkale Turkey 30 H3
Panama *Country* North America 15 K10
Panama Canal Panama 15 K10
Panama City Panama 15 L10
Panama, Gulf of Panama 15 L10
Panuco, R. Mexico 14 G6
Papua New Guinea *Country* Pacific Ocean 42 H5
Paraguay *Country* South America 17 L5
Paraguay, R. South America 17 M5
Paramaribo Surinam 17 M2
Paraná, R. Argentina/Paraguay 17 M6
Paris France 25 L5
Patagonia Argentina 17 K10
Patna India 35 L5
Peace R. Canada 10 G6
Pechora, R. Russian Federation 29 K3
Pecos R. U.S.A. 13 I7
Pegu Burma 38 E4
Peking (Beijing) China 37 K4
Pennsylvania *State* U.S.A. 13 M5
Persian Gulf Middle East 31 M5
Perth Australia 40 E7
Peru *Country* South America 17 K3
Peshawar Pakistan 35 I2
Peter 1st I. *Norwegian territory* Antarctica 9 I6
Petropavlovsk-Kamchatskiy Russian Federation 33 M6
Philadelphia U.S.A. 13 N5
Philippine Trench Pacific Ocean 4 G5
Philippines *Country* Asia 39 J5
Phnom Penh Cambodia 38 G5
Phoenix U.S.A. 12 H7
Phuket I. Thailand 38 E6
Pico *Island* Azores, Atlantic Ocean 24 E9
Pierre U.S.A. 13 J4
Pinang Malaysia 38 F6
Pines, Isle of *Island* Cuba 15 K7
Ping, R. Thailand 38 F3
Pitcairn Islands *U.K. territory* Pacific Ocean 43 P7
Pittsburgh U.S.A. 13 M5
Plate, R. Argentina/Uruguay 17 M7
Plenty, Bay of New Zealand 43 K8
Po, R. Italy 27 J6
Pointe-Noire Congo 20 G4
Poland *Country* Europe 27 M3
Ponta Delgada São Miguel Azores, Atlantic Ocean 24 E9
Pontianak Indonesia 38 H8
Poopó, L. Bolivia 17 L5
Popocatépetl *Mountain* Mexico 14 H7
Port-au-Prince Haiti 15 M7

Port Blair Andaman Islands, Indian Ocean 38 E5
Port Elizabeth South Africa 21 I10
Port-Gentil Gabon 20 F3
Port Louis Mauritius 21 N7
Port Moresby Papua New Guinea 42 H5
Port of Spain Trinidad & Tobago 15 P9
Port Said Egypt 19 K4
Port Sudan Sudan 19 K6
Portland U.S.A. 12 F4
Porto Portugal 25 I8
Pôrto Alegre Brazil 17 N6
Porto-Novo Benin 18 G8
Porto Santo *Island* Madeira Islands, Atlantic Ocean 24 G8
Portugal *Country* Europe 25 I9
Poznań Poland 27 M2
Prague Czech Republic 27 L3
Praia Cape Verde, Atlantic Ocean 18 C7
Prairies *Region* Canada/U.S.A. 10 H7 & 13 I4
Pretoria South Africa 21 I8
Prince Edward Island *Province* Canada 11 M8
Prince of Wales I. Canada 11 I3
Pripet, R. Europe 28 G7
Pripet Marshes *Wetlands* Belorussia 28 G7
Puebla Mexico 14 H7
Puerto Rico *U.S.A. territory* Caribbean Sea 15 N8
Pune India 35 I7
Punta Arenas Chile 17 K10
Pusan South Korea 37 M5
Pyongyang North Korea 37 M4
Pyramid, L. U.S.A. 12 F5
Pyrenees *Mountains* Europe 25 K8

Q

Qaidam Basin China 36 G5
Qandahār Afghanistan 32 E9
Qatar *Country* Asia 31 M7
Qattâra Depression Egypt 19 J4
Qilian Mts. China 36 H4
Qinghai L. China 36 H5
Qinling Range *Mountains* China 37 I6
Qom Iran 31 M4
Quebec Canada 11 M8
Quebec *Province* Canada 11 L7
Queen Charlotte Islands Canada 10 F7
Queen Elizabeth Islands Canada 8 D6 & 10 H2
Queen Maud Land *Region* Antarctica 9 L5
Queensland *State* Australia 41 J5
Quetta Pakistan 34 H3
Quito Ecuador 17 K2

R

Rabat Morocco 18 E3
Raleigh U.S.A. 13 N6
Rangoon Burma 38 E4
Rawalpindi Pakistan 35 I2
Recife Brazil 17 O3
Red R. U.S.A. 13 J7
Red R. Vietnam 38 G2
Reindeer L. Canada 11 I6
Réunion I. *French territory* Indian Ocean 21 M7
Reykjavik Iceland 22 D6
Rhine Gorge Germany 27 J3
Rhine, R. Europe 27 I3
Rhode Island *State* U.S.A. 13 O5
Rhône, R. France/Switzerland 25 M7 & 27 J5
Richmond U.S.A. 13 N6
Riga Latvia 28 G6
Rio de Janeiro Brazil 17 N5
Riyadh Saudi Arabia 31 L7
Rockhampton Australia 41 M5
Rocky Mountains Canada/USA 10 E6 & 12 G3
Romania *Country* Europe 28 G8
Rome Italy 27 K7
Ronne Ice Shelf Antarctica 9 K5
Ross Ice Shelf Antarctica 9 L7
Rotorua New Zealand 43 K9
Rotterdam Netherlands 25 M4
Rub' al Khali *Desert* Saudi Arabia 31 L8

Russian Federation *Country* Asia/Europe 28 F6, 29 I5 & 32 D5
Rwanda *Country* Africa 21 I3
Rybinsk Reservoir Russian Federation 29 I5

S

Sable, Cape Canada 11 M9
Sado *Island* Japan 37 N5
Sahara Desert Africa 18 F5
Sahel *Region* Africa 18 E7
Saimaa, L. Finland 23 O6
St. Helens, Mt. U.S.A. 12 F4
St. John's Canada 11 O8
St. Kitts & Nevis *Country* Caribbean Sea 15 O8
St. Lawrence, Gulf of Canada 11 M8
St. Lawrence R. Canada 11 L8
St. Louis U.S.A. 13 L6
St. Lucia *Country* Caribbean Sea 15 O9
St. Petersburg Russian Federation 28 H5
St. Pierre & Miquelon *French territory* Canada 11 N8
St. Vincent and the Grenadines *Country* Caribbean Sea 15 O9
Saipan Northern Mariana Islands, Pacific Ocean 42 H2
Sakakawea, L. U.S.A. 13 I3
Sakhalin I. Russian Federation 33 L6
Salado, R. Argentina 17 L7
Salar de Uyuni, L. Bolivia 17 L5
Salinas Grandes, L. Argentina 17 L6
Salt Lake City U.S.A. 12 H5
Salton Sea *Lake* U.S.A. 12 G7
Salvador Brazil 17 O4
Salween R. China 36 G6 & 38 F3
Salzburg Austria 27 J8
Samara Russian Federation 29 K6
Samaria Gorge Crete, Greece 28 G10
Samarkand Uzbekistan 32 E8
San Andreas Fault U.S.A. 12 F6
San Antonio U.S.A. 13 J8
San Diego U.S.A. 12 G7
San Francisco U.S.A. 12 F6
San Jorge *Gulf* Argentina 17 L9
San José Costa Rica 15 K10
San Juan Puerto Rico 15 O7
San Marino *Country* Europe 27 K6
San Matías *Gulf* Argentina 17 L8
San Salvador El Salvador 15 J9
San'ā Yemen 31 K9
Santa Fe Argentina 17 M7
Santa Fe U.S.A. 13 I6
Santiago Chile 17 K7
Santiago de Cuba Cuba 15 L7
Santo Domingo Dominican Republic 15 N7
São Francisco, R. Brazil 17 N4
São Miguel *Island* Azores, Atlantic Ocean 24 E9
São Paulo Brazil 17 N6
São Roque *Cape* Brazil 17 O3
São Tomé Sao Tome & Principe 20 F3
Sao Tome & Principe *Country* Africa 20 E3
Saône, R. France 25 M6
Sapporo Japan 37 O4
Sarajevo Bosnia-Herzegovina 28 F8
Sardinia *Italian territory* Mediterranean Sea 27 J8
Sarh Chad 19 I8
Saskatchewan *Province* Canada 11 I7
Saskatchewan R., North Canada 10 G7
Saudi Arabia *Country* Asia 31 K7
Scotland *Region* U.K. 25 J2
Scott Base *Research Station* Antarctica 9 L7
Seattle U.S.A. 12 F3
Seine, R. France 25 L5
Semarang Indonesia 38 H10
Semeru, Mt. Indonesia 39 I10
Sendai Japan 37 O5
Senegal *Country* Africa 18 D7
Senegal, R. Africa 18 D7
Seoul South Korea 37 M5
Severn, R. England, U.K. 25 K4
Severnaya Zemlya *Island group* Russian Federation 8 G6 & 32 G2
Sevilla Spain 25 J10
Seychelles *Country* Indian Ocean 21 L5

Sfax Tunisia 18 H3
Shandong Peninsula China 37 K5
Shanghai China 37 L6
Shannon, R. Republic of Ireland 25 I4
Shebeli, R. Ethiopia/Somalia 19 L8
Sheffield England, U.K. 25 K4
Shenyang China 37 L4
Shetland Islands Scotland, U.K. 25 K1
Shijiazhuang China 37 K5
Shikoku *Island* Japan 37 N6
Shīrāz Iran 31 M5
Siberia Russian Federation 32 G5
Sicily *Island* Italy 27 L10
Sierra de Loarre *Mountains* Spain 25 K8
Sierra Leone *Country* Africa 18 D8
Sierra Madre *Mountains* Guatemala/Mexico 14 F5
Sierra Morena *Mountains* Spain 25 J10
Sierra Nevada *Mountains* Spain 25 K10
Sierra Nevada *Mountains* U.S.A. 12 F5 & 25 K10
Sigirya Sri Lanka 35 K10
Silesian Plateau Poland 27 N3
Simpson Desert Australia 41 I5
Singapore *Country* Asia 38 G8
Sirte, Gulf of Libya 19 I4
Sīstān, L. Iran 31 O5
Sjaelland *Island* Denmark 23 K10
Skopje Macedonia 28 F9
Skovorodno Russian Federation 33 J6
Slovakia *Country* Europe 27 M4
Slovenia *Country* Europe 28 E8
Snake R. U.S.A. 12 G5
Socotra *Island* Yemen 31 M10
Sofia Bulgaria 28 G9
Sogne Fjord Norway 23 I6
Solomon Islands *Country* Pacific Ocean 43 I5
Somalia *Country* Africa 19 L9
Somerset I. Canada 10 J3
Sonoran Desert Mexico/U.S.A. 12 G7, 14 E4
South Africa *Country* Africa 20 H8
South Australia *State* Australia 41 I6
South Carolina *State* U.S.A. 13 M7
South Dakota *State* U.S.A. 13 I4
South Island New Zealand 43 J9
South Korea *Country* Asia 37 M5
South Orkney Islands *U.K. territory* Southern Ocean 9 J4
South Polar Plateau Antarctica 9 L6
South Pole Antarctica 9 L6
South Shetland Islands *U.K. territory* Southern Ocean 9 I4
Southampton I. Canada 11 K5
Southern Alps *Mountains* New Zealand 43 J10
Spain *Country* Europe 25 J8
Sri Lanka *Country* Asia 35 K10
Stanovoy Range *Mountains* Russian Federation 33 J6
Stavanger Norway 23 I8
Stewart I. New Zealand 43 J10
Stockholm Sweden 23 M8
Stor, L. Sweden 23 L5
Strasbourg France 25 N5
Streymoy I. Faeroe Islands, Atlantic Ocean 22 F6
Stuttgart Germany 27 J4
Sudan *Country* Africa 19 J7
Sudd Sudan 19 K8
Sulu Archipelago *Island group* Philippines 39 K6
Sumatra *Island* Indonesia 38 F7
Sungari R. China/Russian Federation 37 M3
Superior, L. Canada/U.S.A. 11 J8 & 13 L3
Surabaya Indonesia 39 I10
Surinam *Country* South America 17 M1
Surtsey I. Iceland 22 D6
Suva Fiji 43 K6
Svalbard *Norwegian territory* Arctic Ocean 8 F8
Sverdrup Islands Canada 11 I2
Swaziland *Country* Africa 21 J8
Sweden *Country* Europe 23 L7
Switzerland *Country* Europe 27 I5
Sydney Australia 41 L7
Syria *Country* Asia 31 J4
Syrian Desert Asia 31 J4
Szczecin Poland 27 L2**

T

Table Mt. South Africa 20 H10
Tabríz Iran 31 L2
Tagus, R. Portugal/Spain 25 K9
Tahiti *Island* French Polynesia, Pacific Ocean 43 N6
Taipei Taiwan 37 L8
Taiwan *Country* Asia 37 L8
Taiyuan China 37 J5
Ta'izz Yemen 31 K10
Tajikistan *Country* Asia 32 E8
Taklamakan Desert China 36 E4
Tallinn Estonia 28 G5
Tamanrasset Oasis Algeria 18 G6
Tampa U.S.A. 13 M8
Tampere Finland 23 N6
Tana, L. Ethiopia 19 L7
Tana, R. Norway 23 N2
Tanami Desert Australia 40 H4
Tanganyika, L. Africa 21 I4
Tangier Morocco 18 E3
Tanzania *Country* Africa 21 I4
Tapajós, R. Brazil 17 M4
Taranto Italy 27 M8
Taranto, Gulf of Italy 27 M8
Tarawa Kiribati, Pacific Ocean 43 J4
Tarim R. China 36 E4
Tashkent Uzbekistan 32 E8
Tasmania *State* Australia 41 K10
Taupo, L. New Zealand 43 K9
Taurus Mts. Turkey 31 H3
Taymyr Peninsula Russian Federation 33 I3
Tbilisi Georgia 29 J9
Tegucigalpa Honduras 15 J9
Tehran Iran 31 M3
Tel Aviv Israel 31 I4
Tenerife *Island* Canary Islands, Atlantic Ocean 24 F9
Tennessee *State* U.S.A. 13 L6
Tennessee R. U.S.A. 13 L7
Terceira *Island* Azores, Atlantic Ocean 24 E8
Texas *State* U.S.A. 13 J7
Thailand *Country* Asia 38 F4
Thailand, Gulf of Thailand 38 F5
Thames, R. England, U.K. 25 K4
Thar Desert India/Pakistan 35 I4
Thessaloniki Greece 28 G9
Thimphu Bhutan 35 N4
Thule Greenland 8 D7
Tianjin China 37 K4
Tiber, R. Italy 27 K7
Tibesti Mountains Chad/Libya 19 I6
Tibet *Region* China 36 F6
Tibet, Plateau of China 36 F6
Tien Shan Mts. China/Kyrgyzstan 36 E4
Tigris, R. Asia 31 K4
Tijuana Mexico 14 D4
Timbuktu Mali 18 F7
Timor *Island* Indonesia 39 L10
Tirana Albania 28 F9
Titicaca, L. Bolivia/Peru 17 L4
Tobakakar Hills *Mountains* Afghanistan/Pakistan 34 H3
Tocantins, R. Brazil 17 N4
Togo *Country* Africa 18 F8
Tokelau *New Zealand territory* Pacific Ocean 43 L5
Tokyo Japan 37 O5
Tomsk Russian Federation 32 G6
Tonga *Country* Pacific Ocean 43 K6
Tonga Trench Pacific Ocean 5 J7
Tongking, Gulf of China/Vietnam 37 J9 & 38 H3
Tônlé, L. Cambodia 38 G5
Toowoomba Australia 41 M6
Topeka U.S.A. 13 K5
Torne, R. Sweden 23 N3
Toronto Canada 11 L9
Torrens, L. Australia 41 I7
Torreón Mexico 14 G5
Torres Strait Australia/Papua New Guinea 41 J1
Tórshavn Streymoy I. Faeroe Islands, Atlantic Ocean 22 F6
Toulouse France 25 L7
Townsville Australia 41 L4
Transantarctic Mountains Antarctica 9 L5
Transylvanian Alps *Mountains* Romania 28 G7
Trieste Italy 27 L6
Trinidad & Tobago *Country* Caribbean Sea 15 P9

Tripoli Libya 18 H4
Tromelin I. *French territory* Indian Ocean 21 M6
Tromsø Norway 23 M2
Trondheim Norway 23 K5
Tunis Tunisia 18 H3
Tunisia *Country* Africa 18 G3
Turin Italy 27 J6
Turkana, L. Ethiopia/Kenya 19 K9 & 21 J2
Turkey *Country* Asia 31 I2
Turkmenistan *Country* Asia 32 D8
Turks & Caicos Islands *U.K. territory* Caribbean Sea 15 M6
Turku Finland 23 N7
Tuvalu *Country* Pacific Ocean 43 K5
Tuz, L. Turkey 31 I3
Tyrol *Mountains* Austria 27 K5

U

Ubangi, R. Central African Republic/Congo 20 G3
Uele, R. Central African Republic/Zaire 21 I2
Uganda *Country* Africa 21 J2
Ujung Pandang Indonesia 39 J9
Ukraine *Country* Europe 29 G7
Ulan Bator Mongolia 33 I7
Ulan-Ude Russian Federation 33 I6
Uliastay Mongolia 32 H7
Uluru (Ayers Rock) *Mountain* Australia 40 H5
Ume, R. Sweden 23 M5
Ungava Bay Canada 11 M6
Ungava Peninsula Canada 11 L6
United Arab Emirates *Country* Asia 31 M7
United Kingdom *Country* Europe 25 K3
United States of America *Country* North America 12-13
Uppsala Sweden 23 M7
Ural Mountains Russian Federation 29 L5 & 32 E5
Ural'sk Kazakhstan 32 D7
Urmia, L. Iran 31 L3
Uruguay *Country* South America 17 M7
Ürümqi China 36 F3
Utah *State* U.S.A. 12 G6
Utrecht Netherlands 25 M4
Uzbekistan *Country* Asia 32 D8

V

Vaasa Finland 23 N5
Vadsø Norway 23 O1
Valencia Spain 25 K9
Valladolid Spain 25 J8
Valletta Malta 27 L10
Van, L. Turkey 31 K2
Vancouver Canada 10 G8
Vancouver I. Canada 10 F8
Väner, L. Sweden 23 K8
Vanuatu *Country* Pacific Ocean 43 I6
Varanger Fjord Norway 23 O1
Vásterås Sweden 23 L7
Vatican City *Country* Rome, Italy 27 K7
Vatnajökull Ice Sheet Iceland 22 D6
Vätter, L. Sweden 23 L8
Vaygach I. Russian Federation 29 L2
Venezuela *Country* South America 17 K1
Venice Italy 27 K6
Verkhoyansk Range *Mountains* Russian Federation 33 J4
Vermont *State* U.S.A. 13 O4
Victoria Seychelles 21 M4
Victoria *State* Australia 41 J8
Victoria Falls *Waterfall* Zambia/Zimbabwe 21 I6
Victoria I. Canada 10 G4
Victoria, L. Africa 21 J3
Victoria Land *Region* Antarctica 9 L7
Vienna Austria 27 M4
Vientiane Laos 38 G3
Vietnam *Country* Asia 38 H4
Vila Vanuatu, Pacific Ocean 43 J6
Vilnius Lithuania 28 G6
Virgin Islands *U.K./U.S.A. territories* Caribbean Sea 15 O7
Virginia *State* U.S.A. 13 N6
Viscount Melville Sound Canada 10 H3
Vistula, R. Poland 27 N2

Vladivostok Russian Federation 33 K8
Volga, R. Russian Federation 29 J7
Vostok *Research station* Antarctica 9 N7

W

Wadi ar Rimah Saudi Arabia 31 J6
Wadi el Milk Sudan 19 J7
Wadi Masilah Yemen 31 L9
Wadi Ruaus Libya 18 H4
Wagga Wagga Australia 41 L8
Wake I. *U.S.A. territory* Pacific Ocean 43 J2
Wales *Region* U.K. 25 J4
Wallis & Futuna *French territory* Pacific Ocean 43 K6
Walvis Bay Namibia 20 G8
Warsaw Poland 27 N2
Washington *State* U.S.A. 12 F3
Washington D.C. U.S.A. 13 N6
Wellington New Zealand 43 K9
Weser, R. Germany 27 J2
West Siberian Plain Russian Federation 32 F5
West Virginia *State* U.S.A. 13 M6
Western Australia *State* Australia 40 G5
Western Ghats *Mountains* India 35 I7
Western Sahara *Disputed territory* Africa 18 D6
Western Samoa *Country* Pacific Ocean 43 L5
White Nile *River* Africa 19 K8
Whitney, Mt. U.S.A. 12 F6
Whyalla Australia 41 I7
Wilhelm, Mt. Papua New Guinea 42 H5
Wilkes Land *Region* Antarctica 9 M8
Windhoek Namibia 20 G7
Windward Passage *Strait* Cuba/Haiti 15 M7
Winnipeg Canada 11 J8
Winnipeg, L. Canada 11 I7
Wisconsin *State* U.S.A. 13 K4
Wollongong Australia 41 L8
Wrangel I. Russian Federation 8 E4 & 33 O4
Wrocław Poland 27 M3
Wuhan China 37 K6
Wyndham Australia 40 G3
Wyoming *State* U.S.A. 12 H4

X

Xi'an China 37 J6
Xingu, R. Brazil 17 M4

Y

Yakutsk Russian Federation 33 K5
Yamal Peninsula Russian Federation 32 E4
Yamoussoukro Ivory Coast 18 E8
Yangtze R. China 36 G6 & 37 K6
Yaoundé Cameroon 18 H9
Yaren Nauru, Pacific Ocean 43 J4
Yekaterinburg Russian Federation 32 E6
Yellow R. China 36 H5 & 37 K5
Yellowknife Canada 10 H5
Yemen *Country* Asia 31 L9
Yenisey, R. Russian Federation 32 G4
Yerevan Armenia 31 K2
Yokohama Japan 37 O5
York, Cape Australia 41 K1
Yucatán Channel Cuba/Mexico 15 J6
Yucatán Peninsula Mexico 15 J7
Yugoslavia *Country* Europe 28 F8
Yukon R. Canada/U.S.A. 10 E6 & 12 D6
Yukon Territory *Province* Canada 10 E5
Yuzhno-Sakhalinsk Russian Federation 33 L7

Z

Zagreb Croatia 28 F8
Zagros Mountains Iran 31 L4
Zaire *Country* Africa 20 G3
Zambezi, R. Africa 21 J6
Zambia *Country* Africa 21 I6
Zamboanga Philippines 39 K6
Zanzibar I. Tanzania 21 K4
Zaragoza Spain 25 K8
Zhengzhou China 37 J5
Zimbabwe *Country* Africa 21 I7
Zurich Switzerland 27 J5

GLOSSARY

Basin A dip, or depression, in the Earth's surface.

Bay A curve in the coastline.

Channel A wide stretch of water linking two areas of sea.

Climate The usual weather of an area.

Coastline The edge of the land, where it meets the sea.

Cold desert A place with low temperatures and very little rain.

Coniferous tree A type of tree, such as a pine, that has leaves shaped like needles.

Continent A vast landmass. The seven continents are Africa, Antarctica, Asia, Australia, Europe, North America and South America.

Coral Tiny sea animals that make chalky skeletons around their bodies. Over time, these skeletons pile up to form a reef.

Current A stream of water that flows through the sea.

Delta A build-up of sand, mud and stones around a river as it enters the sea. A delta may form inland if a river cannot reach the coast.

Drought A long period of time when there is little or no rain.

Dune Sand that the wind has blown into a large mound.

Earthquake A sudden and often violent movement of the Earth's surface.

Equator An imaginary line that runs all the way around the middle of the Earth.

Erosion The gradual wearing away of the land, usually by wind or water.

Fault A large crack in the Earth's surface, or crust, caused by movement under the ground.

Fjord A steep-sided, coastal valley that has been created by ice and flooded by the sea.

Flash flood A sudden, spectacular flood that happens after a very heavy rainstorm.

Geyser A jet of hot water that spurts up from under the ground.

Glacier A huge mass of ice.

Gorge A steep-sided valley that has been created by a river. Deep gorges are called canyons.

Gulf A large, deep bay.

Hot desert A place with high daytime temperatures and very little rain.

Hurricane A storm that begins over oceans in tropical areas. Hurricanes are also known as cyclones.

Isthmus A narrow strip of land between two seas.

Landmass A large area of land surrounded by oceans.

Lava Hot, melted rock.

Mainland The main part of a landmass.

Mountain A place on the Earth's surface which is much higher than a hill.

Oasis A place in the desert where water reaches the surface.

Ocean An enormous body of salty water that is much bigger and deeper than a sea.

Peat bog A wetland where the ground is mostly made up of tightly packed, dead plants.

Peninsula An area of land that juts out into the sea.

Plain A large area of fairly flat land.

Plateau A large, raised area of flat land.

Polar zones The two vast cold regions of the Earth that lie north of the Arctic Circle and south of the Antarctic Circle.

Range A group of hills or mountains.

Rift valley A valley that has formed where the land has fallen down between two faults.

Season A time of year that has a special type of climate, such as winter.

Spit A long, narrow strip of sand and stones that reaches out from the land into the sea.

Stack A tall pillar of rock that stands in coastal waters.

State A part of a country. The United States is made up of 50 states. Australia has six states and two territories. Canada is made up of 12 parts that are known as provinces.

Strait A narrow stretch of water that connects two seas.

Temperate forest Tree-covered areas in the temperate zones. In places where the climate is very wet, temperate rainforests may grow.

Temperate grassland Grass-covered areas in the temperate zones, such as the Prairies in North America and the Steppes in Asia.

Temperate zones The two huge regions of the Earth that lie between the tropical zone and the polar zones.

Territory An area of land, or a town, that belongs to a country.

Tide The rise and fall of the sea, caused by the pull of the Sun and Moon on the water.

Trench A place on the ocean floor where two sections of the Earth's surface meet.

Tropical forest Tree-covered areas in the tropical zone. In places where the climate is very wet, tropical rainforests may grow.

Tropical grassland Grass-covered areas, with scattered trees in the tropical zone. They are also known as savanna.

Tropical zone The hot region of the Earth that lies between the Tropic of Cancer and the Tropic of Capricorn.

Tundra Cold, treeless lands that are mainly found near the ice-covered areas of the Earth.

Typhoon A small, violent storm that often forms in the Pacific Ocean.

Volcano The place where hot, liquid rock breaks through the Earth's crust.

Wadi A dry river valley in a desert. Usually a wadi will only carry water after a flash flood.

Wetland Places, such as bogs and marshes, where water lies on the surface of the land.

Whirlpool A strong, swirling movement in water. It is found at the bottom of a waterfall or where sea currents meet.

Acknowledgments

Geographical Advice:
Andrew Heritage & Roger Bullen
Dr. David R. Green
Illustrations:
Simone End & David Wright
Editorial Assistance:
Margaret Hynes
Design Assistance: Rhonda Fisher
Digital Base Map Production:
Professor Jan-Peter A.L. Muller,
Department of Photogrammetry &
Surveying, University College, London

Picture credits

Bruce Coleman: 15tr, G. Cubitt 20c, 35tc, 39c, F. Erize 9bl, M. Freeman 16bc, S. Krasemann 11tr, H. Lange 40br, H.P. Merten 27cr, D.& M. Plage 19br, Dr. E. Pott 8cl, Mr. Prato title page, 34c, 40bl, J. Shaw 13tr, K. Wothe 22br; **James Davis Travel Photography:** 14bl, 15tl; **Frank Lane Picture Agency:** E.& D. Hosking 20cl, S. McCutcheon 11cr, M. Newman 33br, Silvestris 22cl, W. Wisniewski 22cr; **Robert Harding Picture Library:** 13tr, 19ca, 24crb, 36cb, 38clb, M. H. Black 24c, G. Hellier 37tr, T. Laird 34cl, G. Renner 19tl, front cover cla, R. Richardson 24tr, C. C. D. Tokeley 38bc, A. C. Waltham 36cl; **The Hutchinson Library:** T. E. Clark 11br, R. Francis 39tl, E. Lawrie 17cl, B. Moset 33bc; **The Image Bank:** K. Mori 43br, front cover cla; **Images Colour Library /Horizon:** A. Apse 42cb; **Itar-Tass:** 33tr; **NHPA:** 40cl, G. Gainsborough 16tr, K. Schaffer 16br; **Oxford Scientific Films:** F. Bavendam 41tr; **Pictor International:** front cover tc, 10cl, 20bc, 25tc, 25tr, 25cl, 30cl, 32l, 37br, 42cl; **Picturepoint:** 32br; **Planet Earth Pictures:** Joyce Photographics 42clb; **Donna Rispoli** 13br; **Still Pictures:** C. Caldicott 14bc, E. Parker 18bl; **Tony Stone Images:** 26c, 26cr, 29cr, R. Everts 28c, A. Kearney 17br, D. Nausbaum 12br, B. Parsley 21bc, F. Prenzel 30br; **Survival Anglia Photolibrary:** J. Bennett 9tl; **Telegraph Colour Library:** 26tr; **Colorific!:** B. Boyd 21tr, M. Koene 35br; **Trip:** P. Romter 23tl; **World Pictures:** 28clb; **ZEFA:** Studio Benser 26bc, Damm 30cr, back cover c, 31tl, Heinrich 29bc.

t - **top**   1 - **left**   a - **above**   cb - **centre below**   b - **bottom**   r - **right**   c - **centre**   clb - **centre left below**   crb - **centre right below**

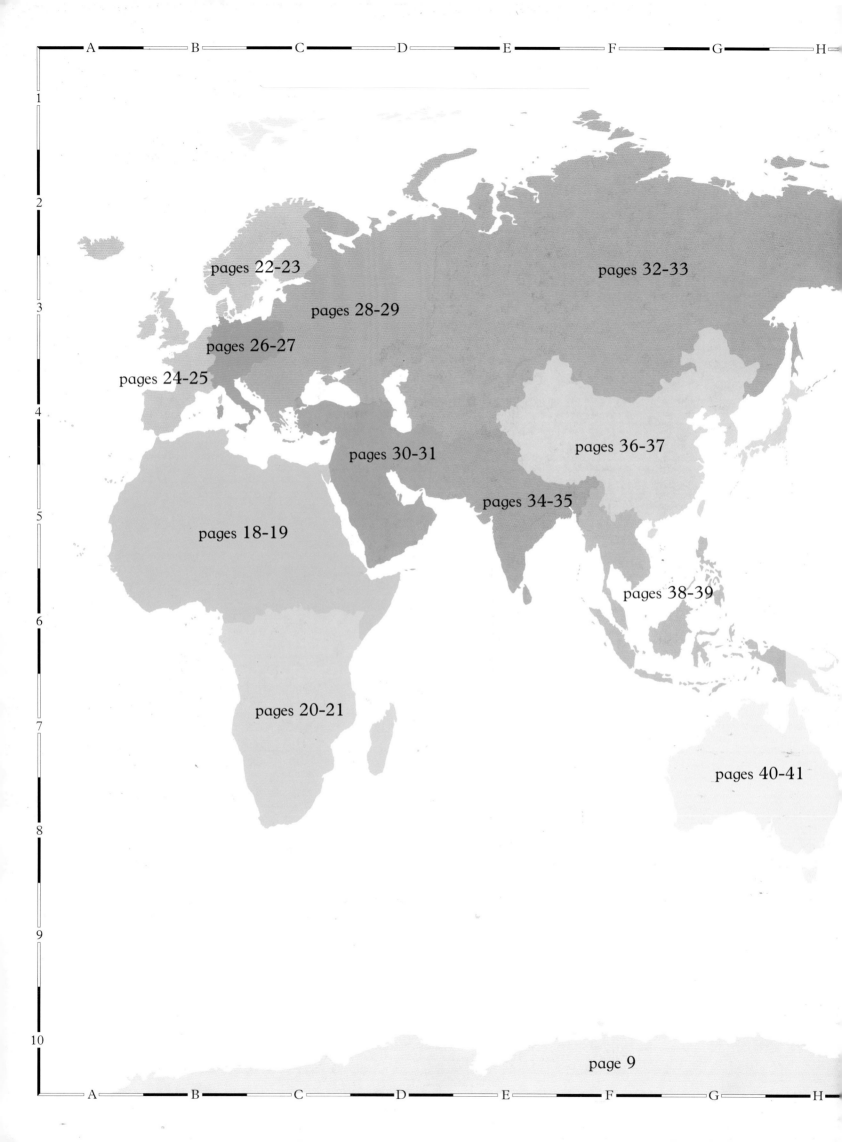

pages 22-23

pages 32-33

pages 28-29

pages 26-27

pages 24-25

pages 30-31

pages 36-37

pages 34-35

pages 18-19

pages 38-39

pages 20-21

pages 40-41

page 9